CURRICULUM ACTIVITIES
FOR GIFTED AND MOTIVATED
ELEMENTARY STUDENTS

CURRICULUM ACTIVITIES FOR GIFTED AND MOTIVATED ELEMENTARY STUDENTS

Edited by

Artie Kamiya and Alan Reiman

PARKER PUBLISHING COMPANY
West Nyack, New York 10995

© 1987 by
Artie Kamiya

10 9 8 7 6 5 4 3 2

Dedicated to children

Library of Congress Cataloging-in-Publication Data

Curriculum activities for gifted and motivated
    elementary students.

    Bibliography: p.
    1. Gifted children—Education—United States.
2. Education, Elementary—United States—
Curricula.
I. Kamiya, Art.   II. Reiman, Alan.
LC3993.9.C87   1987   371.9′5   87-25909

ISBN 0-13-195637-X

PARKER PUBLISHING COMPANY
BUSINESS & PROFESSIONAL DIVISION
A division of Simon & Schuster
West Nyack, New York 10995

Printed in the United States of America

EDITORS AND CONTRIBUTORS

ARTIE KAMIYA has written numerous articles in the area of education and is the author of *Elementary Teacher's Handbook of Indoor and Outdoor Games* (Parker Publishing, 1985). Mr. Kamiya was the physical education teacher at Underwood Elementary School during its first years as a Gifted and Talented Magnet School. Currently, he is a Physical Education Consultant for the North Carolina State Department of Public Instruction, and is the editor of two nationally distributed physical education publications, *The Great Activities Newspaper* and *Gym Dandies*.

ALAN REIMAN has been involved with numerous curriculum development projects, has been an active presenter in the area of early childhood education, and was a Mentor Teacher while at Underwood. He was co-chairperson of North Carolina's "Odyssey of the Mind," a nationally recognized program to encourage problem solving and creative thinking. Mr. Reiman is currently the Supervisor of Student Teachers at Meredith College in Raleigh, North Carolina. He is also working toward his doctorate in Curriculum and Instruction at North Carolina State University.

MARILYN BAILEY has been involved in education as a Gifted and Talented and classroom teacher for 16 years. She has been instrumental in the development of guidelines for Gifted and Talented education within the Wake County School System, and has been a vital and innovative member of the Underwood staff.

MARY DASCOMBE has been teaching for 18 years. An enthusiastic and energetic teacher, she is widely respected for her innovative instructional methods. Ms. Dascombe has also been involved in elementary school curriculum development for the Wake County schools.

BARB ENGRAM has been involved as a Gifted and Talented and classroom teacher for 16 years. Ms. Engram has developed an imaginative and effective curriculum related to Black History. She has written several educational articles and has been published by Good Apple Publications. The Underwood staff selected Ms. Engram as its "Teacher of the Year."

DON FAIRMAN's love for children has been repeatedly acknowledged and appreciated by both staff and parents during the two years he has been at Underwood. His flair for "hands-on" learning was recently reflected in his latest project: a six-foot plywood model of a Tyrannosaurus Rex that could be assembled by his kindergarten students.

MARY ANN GIEZMA has been teaching for eight years. Her dedication to the teaching profession was recognized in her selection to a special pilot program at the Center for the Advancement of Teaching at Western Carolina University.

CAROL GREGORY's creativity is a constant source of inspiration. As the Media Specialist at Underwood, she has developed numerous student projects in research skills. A past nominee for a state-wide award for teacher innovation/creativity, Ms. Gregory is also involved with teaching Spanish (she spent three years in South America with the Peace Corps) and computer education.

HELEN JONES has contributed much to the Underwood staff through her concern that each student learn practical and worthwhile skills and knowledge. An innovative fourth grade teacher, she has been responsible for numerous projects aimed at building a better student awareness of "buying and selling" economics.

PAM KINGERY's enthusiasm has meant much to her students and staff. She turned Underwood's front lawn into a French café complete with French-speaking waiters and waitresses and all the necessary accoutrements. Ms. Kingery was recently asked to chair a committee responsible for state-wide instruction in French.

MAZIE LESTER has 24 years of teaching experience. Her dedication is evident in her daily interactions with her second-graders. Most recently, she has coordinated efforts to implement the Success in Reading and Writing Program at Underwood.

BETTY MACKIE is working on a master's degree in literature at North Carolina State University. During her three years at Underwood, she has taught several courses that reflect her love of literature. One example is an elective called "Novels and Short Stories," which features the work of Shakespeare.

LINDA STIPE has been involved in writing the curriculum for the Gifted and Talented Magnet School Program for the Wake County schools. While at Underwood, Ms. Stipe taught a first/second grade combination class. She is currently serving as the Principal at Baucom Elementary School in Raleigh, North Carolina.

BARBARA TIMBERLAKE's work with Underwood and the Wake County School System spans 25 years. She is an advocate for improving student writing skills and assisted in the development and implementation of the *Developmental Skills Writing Guide*. A former Mentor Teacher at Underwood, Ms. Timberlake is currently an Assistant Principal at Carnage Middle School in Raleigh, North Carolina.

PHILLIP VINCENT serves as a part-time Gifted and Talented resource teacher. He is the co-author of a nationally distributed philosophy curriculum for grades 4–12. Mr. Vincent is working on his doctorate in Curriculum and Instruction at North Carolina State University.

BONNIE WAGSTAFF has been teaching for five years, during which time she has earned the reputation as an energetic and creative teacher. Her class recently presented a program called "Old MacDonald's Farm," which incorporated music, drama, and costumes.

LYNN WILLIAMS was the Gifted and Talented resource teacher at Underwood. Having built a reputation as a "doer," she has written various articles in the area of Gifted and Talented education and has demonstrated exceptional leadership in her roles as both state and regional director of the "Odyssey of the Mind" competitions. Ms. Williams is currently an Assistant Principal in charge of Curriculum and Instruction at York Elementary School in Raleigh, North Carolina.

ABOUT THIS BOOK

Curriculum Activities for Gifted and Motivated Elementary Students is the result of a group of teachers' commitment to the nurturance of those students who have shown high academic potential. The 166 activities in this practical resource book have been carefully selected to provide your gifted and motivated elementary students with interesting and challenging learning experiences.

The activities in this book are designed with you in mind, particularly if you are interested in dramatically reducing planning time on proven successful strategies for helping children go beyond basic competency levels. For example, you will help your students:

- develop high levels of skill in structured science activities and experiences
- gain new insights as they explore the uses of mathematics in today's society
- acquire the skills necessary for making sound decisions through the use of logic
- utilize the written and spoken word through exciting activities in grammar, literature, and drama
- explore their own unique qualities, as well as their families', and others'
- develop better access to imaginative and exciting research techniques

Curriculum Activities for Gifted and Motivated Elementary Students is divided into seven sections that help your students go beyond basic competency levels:

1. *Discovering Myself and the World Around Me* offers 23 activities that will teach your students more about themselves and the different cultures of the world. For example, students will learn how to plan, develop, and operate a French café—preparing menus and dinners, and acting as waiters and waitresses.

2. *Math Amazing* consists of 46 activities that set the stage for students wishing to explore such areas of mathematics as architecture, consumerism, banking, and metrics.

3. *Writing Wisely* provides your students with 18 activities for constructing effective and creative compositions—from imaginative approaches to poetry writing to learning the writing process. Included are writing projects for each month of the school year.

4. *Research Roundup* gives students a firm footing in the fundamentals of doing library research. The 25 activities in this section will take your students through such areas as the Dewey Decimal Classification system, autobiographies, and the card catalog system.

5. *Logic and You* includes 14 activities that will help enhance your students' thinking and reasoning skills. For example, your students will be introduced to fallacies of reasoning and the logic of rules.

6. *The Glad Scientist* will delight your students as well as pique their curiosities. The 24 activities will help develop your students' thinking skills and nurture their inquiring minds through such activities as dramatizing the demise of dinosaurs or exploring the five senses.

7. *Viewpoints* introduces your students to geography. Through this section's 16 activities, your students will become geographers and, once knowledgeable, will apply their skills to creative geography problems.

Each section contains full-page activity sheets and patterns you can reproduce immediately and as many times as needed for use with your students. Also included at the end of each section are additional topics you can explore that relate to that particular area and a bibliography for further study. A special feature of *Curriculum Activities for Gifted and Motivated Elementary Students* is the Skills Index that lists the particular skills taught by each activity. It will help you select activities for individuals based on their areas of need or interest.

Remember that one of our most important tasks is to help students identify their special talents and encourage them to use their gifts to the best of their abilities. The many time-tested and innovative ideas in *Curriculum Activities for Gifted and Motivated Elementary Students* will help you do just that!

Artie Kamiya

Alan Reiman

ACKNOWLEDGMENTS

A special tribute was paid to the staff of Underwood Elementary School. *Instructor* magazine, a nationally recognized publication, selected Underwood to be a part of its "A+ Schools" honor roll of effective and model school programs. "What is special of Underwood," states teacher David Wall in the magazine's May 1986 issue, "is that if children find a gift they enjoy—whether it is art, photography, or dramatics—we want them to go for it. We encourage them in every way!" This statement is also reflective of the many long hours of effort placed in the production of this special resource. The editors want to thank these teachers for their hard work and esprit de corps!

Peggy Churn, Underwood's principal and guiding light, is thanked for her support and encouragement of this project.

We appreciate The Riverside Publishing Company's cooperation in granting us permission to reprint the three maps in activity 7-11, "Geographical Bingo."

Finally, the editors are grateful for their spouses, Elizabeth Kamiya and Evelyn Reiman. Their love, patience, and understanding were priceless during the process of preparing this book.

A.K.

A.R.

TABLE OF CONTENTS

About This Book ix
Skills Index xxv

Section 1
DISCOVERING MYSELF
AND THE WORLD AROUND ME 1

It's Me, Only Me! 4

    1-1 Likes and Dislikes (K-3) **4**

    1-2 Motto Me (K-3) **5**

    1-3 All Right! (K-3) **6**

    1-4 Wow, Are You Sure? (K-3) **6**

Discovering Leadership 8

    1-5 Off to the Stars (K-3) **8**

    1-6 Starshare (K-3) **10**

    1-7 Starpower (K-3) **10**

The French Café 11

    1-8 What's It All About (4-6) **11**

    1-9 Surveying the Situation (4-6) **12**

    1-10 Setting the Scene (4-6) **13**

    1-11 Now, Set the Mood (4-6) **13**

    1-12 Spread the Word (4-6) **14**

1-13 The Menu (4-6) **14**

1-14 The Art of French Cooking (4-6) **15**

1-15 If Only Tables Could Talk (4-6) **16**

1-16 Cooking with Chef Jacques (4-6) **17**

1-17 The Countdown (4-6) **17**

1-18 We're Open! (4-6) **18**

Black American History   **19**

1-19 The Afro Game (4-6) **19**

Imagination Games   **28**

1-20 Oranges Everywhere (K-3) **28**

1-21 Orange Essence (K-3) **29**

1-22 Adjectives Abound (K-3) **30**

1-23 What If? (K-3) **30**

*Research Topics for Further Study of "Discovering Myself and
the World Around Me"*   **32**

Bibliography for "Discovering Myself and the World Around Me"   **32**

Section 2
MATH AMAZING 33

Budgeting and Banking   **38**

2-1 Money Talks (4-6) **38**

2-2 Budgeting (4-6) **43**

Take Me to Your Liter 'Cause I Want to Meter   **46**

    2-3   *The History of Metric (4-6)* **46**

    2-4   *Metric Map (4-6)* **46**

    2-5   *Metric Scavenger Hunt (4-6)* **47**

    2-6   *I Want to Meter (4-6)* **49**

    2-7   *Decimeter Jump (K-3)* **49**

    2-8   *Metric Measuring Mania (4-6)* **50**

    2-9   *Residential Design (4-6)* **51**

Consumer Math   **52**

    2-10   *Food Forum (4-6)* **52**

    2-11   *Fruit Search (4-6)* **52**

    2-12   *Ad Vantage (4-6)* **53**

    2-13   *Goods and Services (4-6)* **54**

    2-14   *Let's Eat Out! (4-6)* **54**

    2-15   *What's In It? (4-6)* **55**

Environmental Geometry   **56**

    2-16   *Shapes Alive Braindrawing (K-3)* **56**

    2-17   *Shape Scientists (K-3)* **57**

    2-18   *Outdoor Wonderland (K-3)* **59**

    2-19   *Shape Artistry (K-3)* **60**

    2-20   *Geometric Recursion (K-3)* **60**

    2-21   *Shapes Recipes (K-3)* **61**

    2-22   *Sharing Recipes (K-3)* **61**

    2-23   *Repeating Patterns Collage (K-3)* **62**

2-24   *Shapes Movements (K-3)* **62**

2-25   *Fractals (K-3)* **63**

2-26   *Playground Geometry I (K-3)* **63**

2-27   *Playground Geometry II (K-3)* **64**

Numeralonics   **65**

2-28   *Make a Logo (K-3)* **65**

2-29   *Logo Rodeo (K-3)* **66**

2-30   *The Nature of Number/Numeral (K-3)* **66**

2-31   *Numeral Time Machine (K-3)* **67**

2-32   *I Got the System (K-3)* **68**

Math Happenings   **69**

2-33   *Measurement Monday (K-3)* **70**

2-34   *Student Teaching Tuesday (K-3)* **70**

2-35   *Workers' Wednesday (K-3)* **71**

2-36   *Try to Guess Thursday (K-3)* **71**

2-37   *Far Away Friday (K-3)* **71**

2-38   *Math-Go-Round (K-3)* **72**

2-39   *Calculator Chatter and Babbles (4-6)* **72**

Architecture Around Us   **74**

2-40   *What's Happening Here? (K-3)* **74**

2-41   *Pulling Apart an Idea (K-3)* **75**

2-42   *Chairperson (K-3)* **76**

2-43   *By Way of the Bridge (K-3)* **77**

2-44   *Load It On...1 (K-3)* **78**

2-45   *Load It On...2 (K-3)* **78**

2-46   *Load It On...3 (K-3)* **79**

Research Topics for Further Study of "Math Amazing" 82

Bibliography for "Math Amazing" 82

Section 3
WRITING WISELY 83

The Writing Process: A Primer for Teachers 85

    3-1   Prewriting (4-6) **85**

    3-2   Writing (4-6) **86**

    3-3   Editing/Revising (4-6) **86**

    3-4   Evaluation (4-6) **88**

Brew, Balloons, and Doodles 89

    3-5   Witch's Brew (4-6) **89**

    3-6   Balloons, Balloons, Balloons!!! (4-6) **90**

    3-7   Describe a Doodle (4-6) **91**

Creative Writing: A+ 93

    3-8   September—Success in the UFL (4-6) **93**

    3-9   October—Thoughts in the Cave (4-6) **96**

    3-10   November—Story Starters (4-6) **98**

    3-11   December—What's in a Card? (4-6) **100**

    3-12   Spring in January (4-6) **101**

    3-13   February—Valid Valentines (4-6) **102**

    3-14   March—Soaring Ideas (4-6) **102**

    3-15   April—Crack Me Open (4-6) **103**

    3-16   May—Blooming Ideas (4-6) **105**

3-17   June—Creative Writing Plug-Ins (4-6) **106**

3-18   Parts of Speech File Fun (4-6) **106**

Research Topics for Further Study of "Writing Wisely"   **111**

Bibliography for "Writing Wisely"   **114**

Section 4
RESEARCH ROUNDUP   115

Do We Know Dewey?   118

4-1   Class Feet (K-3) **118**

4-2   Who Needs It? (K-3) **119**

4-3   The Whole Is the Sum of Its Parts (K-3) **121**

4-4   Scavenger Hunt (K-3) **124**

4-5   Match-U (K-3) **127**

4-6   Betcha' Know or Dewey Lottery (K-3) **130**

4-7   Dramatized Dewey (4-6) **130**

4-8   Make-a-Monster (4-6) **131**

The Hidden History of Heroes   135

4-9   Heroes in Our Midst (4-6) **135**

4-10   The Provocative Question (4-6) **137**

4-11   Setting Up the Interview (4-6) **138**

4-12   The Interview (4-6) **138**

4-13   Production Time (4-6) **139**

4-14   Collective Biography (4-6) **140**

Playing Your Cards...Right!   **141**

4-15   Anatomy of a Card (4-6)   **141**

4-16   One Equals Three (4-6)   **143**

4-17   Number Pull-Eeze (4-6)   **143**

4-18   Copy Cats! (4-6)   **146**

4-19   Create a Card (4-6)   **150**

Dictionary Delight   **152**

4-20   The "Guide"-ing Light (4-6)   **152**

4-21   "Guide" to Math (4-6)   **153**

4-22   Two-Clue Teasers (4-6)   **154**

4-23   A Nu Lang'-Gwij (4-6)   **156**

4-24   Help the Turkey Trot (4-6)   **157**

4-25   In Other Words (4-6)   **160**

Topics for Further Study of "Research Roundup"   **161**

Bibliography for "Research Roundup"   **161**

Section 5
LOGIC AND YOU   163

Fallacies of Reasoning   **165**

5-1   Appeal to Pity (4-6)   **165**

5-2   Appeal to Force (4-6)   **166**

5-3   Appeal to Authority (4-6)   **167**

5-4   Appeal to Popularity (4-6) **167**

5-5   Appeal to Abuse (4-6) **168**

Flow Charts   **170**

5-6   Cause—What Effect? (4-6) **170**

5-7   Where's the Water? (4-6) **171**

5-8   Flowing Ideas (4-6) **171**

5-9   Implications Flow Chart (4-6) **172**

Rules Around Us   **175**

5-10   Rules at School (4-6) **175**

5-11   Rules at Home (4-6) **176**

5-12   Rules in the Community (4-6) **177**

5-13   Rule of Thumb (4-6) **178**

5-14   Energy-Saving Device (4-6) **178**

Research Topics for Further Study of "Logic and You"   **183**

Bibliography for "Logic and You"   **183**

Section 6
THE GLAD SCIENTIST 185

Dinosaurs, Dinosaurs!   **188**

6-1   Dinosaur Book (K-3) **188**

6-2   I've Got a Dinosaur on My Back (K-3) **196**

6-3   Dinosaur Jeopardy (K-3) **196**

6-4   Love Those Bones (K-3) **196**

6-5   *Gone is Gone (4-6)*   **197**

6-6   *They Are Known by Their Bones (4-6)*   **198**

The Human Machine   199

6-7   *The Human Body (K-3)*   **199**

6-8   *Body Awareness (K-3)*   **208**

6-9   *Mixed-Up Body (K-3)*   **208**

Exploring Your Senses   209

6-10   *La Premiere Cochon ("The # 1 Pig" in French) (K-3)*   **209**

6-11   *The Feel of Things (K-3)*   **213**

6-12   *Henrietta and Taste (K-3)*   **214**

6-13   *Henrietta and Smelling (K-3)*   **216**

6-14   *Hearing and Henrietta (K-3)*   **217**

6-15   *Seeing with Henrietta (K-3)*   **218**

Ecology and Me   220

6-16   *Weave a Web (K-3)*   **220**

6-17   *Ecology and Language Arts (K-3)*   **221**

6-18   *A Pinch of This, a Dab of That (K-3)*   **222**

The Wonder of Wildflowers   223

6-19   *Wildflowers? (K-3)*   **223**

6-20   *Data Sharing (K-3)*   **224**

6-21   *Wildflowers and Mythology (K-3)*   **224**

6-22   *Walk On (K-3)*   **225**

6-23   *Compare and Contrast (K-3)*   **225**

6-24   *What's in a Name? (K-3)*   **226**

Research Topics for Further Study of "The Glad Scientist"   **227**

Bibliography for "The Glad Scientist"   **227**

Section 7
VIEWPOINTS   229

Becoming Geographers   **231**

7-1   *Hocus, Pocus, Focus (4-6)*   **231**

7-2   *Touch Mapping (4-6)*   **235**

7-3   *Visions (4-6)*   **235**

7-4   *Treasure Hunt (4-6)*   **235**

Rearranging Our World   **237**

7-5   *Cityscape (K-3)*   **237**

7-6   *All About School (4-6)*   **238**

7-7   *Creator (4-6)*   **238**

7-8   *Things Would Be Different If??? (4-6)*   **239**

7-9   *Going Back in Time (4-6)*   **240**

Using Geography   **242**

7-10   *Name That Continent (K-3)*   **242**

7-11   *Geographical Bingo (4-6)*   **243**

7-12   *Map Fluency (4-6)*   **247**

7-13   *This Is the Land That "Jack" Built (4-6)*   **249**

Applied Geography 250

7-14   *Planet X (4-6)*   **250**

7-15   *The Great (Fill in Your State's Nickname) Race (4-6)*   **251**

7-16   *The ABC's of World Travel (4-6)*   **251**

Research Topics for Further Study of "Viewpoints"   **253**

Bibliography for "Viewpoints"   **253**

SKILLS INDEX

Skills

Activity Title and Grade Level	CLASSIFYING	CODING	COLLECTING DATA	COMPARING	CONTRASTING	CRITICIZING	HYPOTHESIZING	IMAGINING	INTERPRETING DATA	LOOKING FOR ASSUMPTIONS	OBSERVING	ORGANIZING DATA	PREDICTING	PROBLEM SOLVING	SUMMARIZING
1-1 Likes and Dislikes (K-3)	X		X									X			
1-2 Motto Me (K-3)								X							
1-3 All Right! (K-3)														X	
1-4 Wow, Are You Sure? (K-3)			X						X						
1-5 Off to the Stars (K-3)									X						
1-6 Starshare (K-3)				X							X				
1-7 Starpower (K-3)														X	
1-8 What It's All About (4-6)			X												
1-9 Surveying the Situation (4-6)			X											X	
1-10 Setting the Scene (4-6)								X				X			
1-11 Now, Set the Mood (4-6)											X			X	
1-12 Spread the Word (4-6)			X			X						X		X	
1-13 The Menu (4-6)				X							X				
1-14 The Art of French Cooking (4-6)	X		X									X			
1-15 If Only Tables Could Talk (4-6)									X						
1-16 Cooking with Chef Jacques (4-6)											X				
1-17 The Countdown (4-6)	X					X									
1-18 We're Open! (4-6)						X						X			

SKILLS INDEX

Skills

Activity Title and Grade Level	CLASSIFYING	CODING	COLLECTING DATA	COMPARING	CONTRASTING	CRITICIZING	HYPOTHESIZING	IMAGINING	INTERPRETING DATA	LOOKING FOR ASSUMPTIONS	OBSERVING	ORGANIZING DATA	PREDICTING	PROBLEM SOLVING	SUMMARIZING
1-19 The Afro Game (4-6)			X						X	X		X			
1-20 Oranges Everywhere (K-3)								X							
1-21 Oranges Essence (K-3)								X							
1-22 Adjectives Abound (K-3)								X							
1-23 What If (K-3)								X							
2-1 Money Talks (4-6)			X									X	X		
2-2 Budgeting (4-6)												X	X		
2-3 The History of Metric (4-6)			X												
2-4 Metric Map (4-6)			X									X			
2-5 Metric Scavenger Hunt (4-6)			X									X			
2-6 I Want to Meter (4-6)		X		X											
2-7 Decimeter Jump (K-3)				X							X				
2-8 Metric Measuring Mania (4-6)			X	X							X	X			
2-9 Residential Design (4-6)			X								X	X			
2-10 Food Forum (4-6)	X							X							
2-11 Fruit Search (4-6)			X								X	X	X		
2-12 Ad Vantage (4-6)			X	X					X			X			
2-13 Goods and Services (4-6)		X							X					X	X
2-14 Let's Eat Out! (4-6)		X							X	X					

SKILLS INDEX

Skills

Activity Title and Grade Level	CLASSIFYING	CODING	COLLECTING DATA	COMPARING	CONTRASTING	CRITICIZING	HYPOTHESIZING	IMAGINING	INTERPRETING DATA	LOOKING FOR ASSUMPTIONS	OBSERVING	ORGANIZING DATA	PREDICTING	PROBLEM SOLVING	SUMMARIZING
2-15 What's In It? (4-6)			X								X	X			
2-16 Shapes Alive Braindrawing (K-3)											X				
2-17 Shape Scientists (K-3)			X									X			
2-18 Outdoor Wonderland (K-3)			X									X			
2-19 Shape Artistry (K-3)		X													
2-20 Geometric Recursion (K-3)		X	X								X	X		X	
2-21 Shapes Recipes (K-3)								X							
2-22 Sharing Recipes (K-3									X					X	
2-23 Repeating Patterns Collage (K-3)	X										X				
2-24 Shapes Movements (K-3)		X						X						X	
2-25 Fractals (K-3)	X	X									X				
2-26 Playround Geometry I (K-3)								X						X	
2-27 Playground Geometry II (K-3)							X	X						X	
2-28 Make a Logo (K-3)								X						X	
2-29 Logo Rodeo (K-3)				X	X										
2-30 The Nature of Number/ Numeral (K-3)				X	X										
2-31 Numeral Time Machine (K-3)				X				X	X		X				

xxvii

SKILLS INDEX

Skills

Activity Title and Grade Level	CLASSIFYING	CODING	COLLECTING DATA	COMPARING	CONTRASTING	CRITICIZING	HYPOTHESIZING	IMAGINING	INTERPRETING DATA	LOOKING FOR ASSUMPTIONS	OBSERVING	ORGANIZING DATA	PREDICTING	PROBLEM SOLVING	SUMMARIZING
2-32 I Got the System (K-3)														X	
2-33 Measurement Monday (K-3)			X	X							X	X			
2-34 Student Teaching Tuesday (K-3)									X					X	
2-35 Workers' Wednesday (K-3)									X						
2-36 Try to Guess Thursday (K-3)							X				X				
2-37 Far Away Friday (K-3)			X					X				X			
2-38 Math-Go-Round (K-3)			X						X			X			
2-39 Calculator Chatter and Babbles (K-3)			X						X			X			
2-40 What's Happening Here (K-3)		X										X			
2-41 Pulling Apart an Idea (K-3)				X								X			
2-42 Chairperson (K-3)							X	X				X			
2-43 By Way of the Bridge (K-3)		X		X					X			X		X	
2-44 Load It On...1 (K-3)									X			X			
2-45 Load It On...2 (K-3)			X				X		X			X	X		
2-46 Load It On...3 (K-3)			X	X					X			X		X	X
3-1 Prewriting (4-6)			X									X			
3-2 Writing (4-6)	X														X
3-3 Editing/Revising (4-6)	X					X									
3-4 Evaluating (4-6)				X		X			X						
3-5 Witch's Brew (4-6)	X		X			X		X				X			

SKILLS INDEX

Activity Title and Grade Level	CLASSIFYING	CODING	COLLECTING DATA	COMPARING	CONTRASTING	CRITICIZING	HYPOTHESIZING	IMAGINING	INTERPRETING DATA	LOOKING FOR ASSUMPTIONS	OBSERVING	ORGANIZING DATA	PREDICTING	PROBLEM SOLVING	SUMMARIZING
3-6 Balloons, Balloons, Balloons!!! (4-6)	X		X	X								X			
3-7 Describe a Doodle (4-6)			X	X		X						X			
3-8 September—Success in UFL (4-6)	X		X					X				X			
3-9 October—Thoughts in the Cave (4-6)							X	X		X					
3-10 November—Story Starters (4-6)							X	X		X					
3-11 December—What's in a Card (4-6)							X	X		X					
3-12 Spring in January (4-6)	X							X							
3-13 February—Valid Valentines (4-6)						X		X							
3-14 March—Soaring Ideas (4-6)			X	X		X		X				X			
3-15 April—Crack Me Open (4-6)	X			X			X								
3-16 May—Blooming Ideas (4-6)			X					X				X			
3-17 June—Creative Writing Plug-Ins (4-6)			X					X				X			
3-18 Parts of Speech File Fun (4-6)	X		X					X				X			
4-1 Class Feet (K-3)	X						X								
4-2 Who Needs It? (K-3)	X		X	X											
4-3 The Whole Is the Sum of Its Parts (K-3)				X					X						

SKILLS INDEX

Activity Title and Grade Level	CLASSIFYING	CODING	COLLECTING DATA	COMPARING	CONTRASTING	CRITICIZING	HYPOTHESIZING	IMAGINING	INTERPRETING DATA	LOOKING FOR ASSUMPTIONS	OBSERVING	ORGANIZING DATA	PREDICTING	PROBLEM SOLVING	SUMMARIZING
4-4 Scavenger (K-3)			X									X			
4-5 Match-U (K-3)				X											
4-6 Betcha' Know or Dewey Lottery (K-3)			X				X			X		X			
4-7 Dramatized Dewey (4-6)							X							X	
4-8 Make-a-Monster (4-6)			X												
4-9 Heroes in Our Midst (4-6)			X	X								X			
4-10 The Provocative Question (4-6)			X					X						X	
4-11 Setting Up the Interview (4-6)												X			
4-12 The Interview (4-6)			X												
4-13 Production Time (4-6)	X											X			X
4-14 Collective Biography (4-6)												X			
4-15 Anatomy of a Card (4-6)	X				X						X				
4-16 One Equals Three (4-6)					X				X						
4-17 Number Pull-Eeze (4-6)			X								X	X			
4-18 Copy Cats! (4-6)			X									X			
4-19 Create a Card (4-6)					X							X			
4-20 The "Guide"-ing Light (4-6)		X									X				
4-21 "Guide" to Match (4-6)												X			
4-22 Two-Clue Teasers (4-6)												X			

SKILLS INDEX

Skills

Activity Title and Grade Level	CLASSIFYING	CODING	COLLECTING DATA	COMPARING	CONTRASTING	CRITICIZING	HYPOTHESIZING	IMAGINING	INTERPRETING DATA	LOOKING FOR ASSUMPTIONS	OBSERVING	ORGANIZING DATA	PREDICTING	PROBLEM SOLVING	SUMMARIZING
4-23 A Nu Lang'-Gwij (4-6)						X					X				
4-24 Help the Turkey Trot (4-6)		X							X					X	
4-25 In Other Words (4-6)			X	X											
5-1 Apeal to Pity (4-6)						X			X	X					
5-2 Appeal to Force (4-6)						X			X	X					
5-3 Appeal to Authority (4-6)						X			X	X					
5-4 Appeal to Popularity (4-6)						X			X	X					
5-5 Appeal to Abuse (4-6)						X			X	X					
5-6 Cause—What Effect? (4-6)							X							X	
5-7 Where's the Water? (4-6)							X								
5-8 Flowing Ideas (4-6)	X	X		X											
5-9 Implications Flow Chart (4-6)		X				X	X								
5-10 Rules at School (4-6)						X			X						
5-11 Rules at Home (4-6)						X			X						
5-12 Rules in the Community (4-6)						X			X						
5-13 Rule of Thumb (4-6)						X			X						
5-14 Energy-Saving Device (4-6)					X	X			X					X	
6-1 Dinosaur Book (K-3)			X									X			X
6-2 I've Got a Dinosaur on My Back (K-3)	X			X						X				X	

SKILLS INDEX

Activity Title and Grade Level	CLASSIFYING	CODING	COLLECTING DATA	COMPARING	CONTRASTING	CRITICIZING	HYPOTHESIZING	IMAGINING	INTERPRETING DATA	LOOKING FOR ASSUMPTIONS	OBSERVING	ORGANIZING DATA	PREDICTING	PROBLEM SOLVING	SUMMARIZING
6-3 Dinosaur Jeopardy (K-3)	X								X						
6-4 Love Those Bones (K-3)			X	X							X				
6-5 Gone Is Gone (4-6)							X	X		X					
6-6 They Are Known by Their Bones (4-6)	X										X				
6-7 The Human Body (K-3)									X		X	X			
6-8 Body Awareness (K-3)											X				
6-9 Mixed-Up Body (K-3)											X				
6-10 La Premiere Cochon (The #1 Pig) (K-3)								X			X				
6-11 The Feel of Things (K-3)			X				X				X	X			
6-12 Henrietta and Taste (K-3)				X							X				
6-13 Henrietta and Smelling (K-3)									X		X				
6-14 Hearing and Henrietta (K-3)									X		X				
6-15 Seeing with Henrietta (K-3)									X		X				
6-16 Weave a Web (K-3)							X	X	X	X					
6-17 Ecology and Language Arts (K-3)									X						
6-18 A Pinch of This, A Dab of That (K-3)								X	X						
6-19 Wildflowers? (K-3)			X									X			
6-20 Data Sharing (K-3)															X
6-21 Wildflowers and Mythology (K-3)							X					X		X	

SKILLS INDEX

Skills

Activity Title and Grade Level	CLASSIFYING	CODING	COLLECTING DATA	COMPARING	CONTRASTING	CRITICIZING	HYPOTHESIZING	IMAGINING	INTERPRETING DATA	LOOKING FOR ASSUMPTIONS	OBSERVING	ORGANIZING DATA	PREDICTING	PROBLEM SOLVING	SUMMARIZING
6-22 Walk On (K-3)			X								X				
6-23 Compare and Contrast (K-3)				X	X										
6-24 What's in a Name? (K-3)								X		X					
7-1 Hocus, Pocus, Focus (4-6)			X								X	X			
7-2 Touch Mapping (4-6)			X						X		X	X			
7-3 Visions (4-6)			X									X	X		
7-4 Treasure Hunt (4-6)									X				X		
7-5 Cityscape (K-3)			X					X	X			X			
7-6 All About School (4-6)			X						X		X			X	
7-7 Creator (4-6)			X				X		X			X		X	
7-8 Things Would Be Different If??? (4-6)			X					X	X			X			
7-9 Going Back in Time (4-6)								X	X						
7-10 Name That Continent (K-3)														X	
7-11 Geographical Bingo (4-6)			X						X			X			
7-12 Map Fluency (4-6)	X											X			
7-13 This Is the Land That "Jack" Built (4-6)	X											X			
7-14 Planet X (4-6)		X						X						X	
7-15 The Great (Fill in Your State's Nickname) Race (4-6)													X	X	
7-16 The ABC's of World Travel (4-6)			X									X		X	

Section 1

DISCOVERING MYSELF AND THE WORLD AROUND ME

This section provides experiences that will help your students learn more about themselves and the different cultures of the world. Your students will develop an awareness of who they are, how they are alike, and how they are different. They will journey from their own personal world of "likes and dislikes" to experiencing the exciting flavor of other cultures…from a French café to the contributions of Black Americans.

ACTIVITY TITLE AND GRADE LEVEL	SKILLS USED
It's Me, Only Me!	
1-1 Likes and Dislikes (K-3)	classifying; collecting and organizing data
1-2 Motto Me (K-3)	imagining
1-3 All Right! (K-3)	problem solving
1-4 Wow, Are You Sure? (K-3)	collecting data; interpreting
Discovering Leadership	
1-5 Off to the Stars (K-3)	interpreting
1-6 Starshare (K-3)	observing; comparing
1-7 Starpower (K-3)	problem solving

ACTIVITY TITLE AND GRADE LEVEL	SKILLS USED

The French Café

1-8	What It's All About (4-6)	collecting data
1-9	Surveying the Situation (4-6)	problem solving; collecting data
1-10	Setting the Scene (4-6)	imagining; organizing data
1-11	Now, Set the Mood (4-6)	observing; problem solving
1-12	Spread the Word (4-6)	problem solving; criticizing; collecting and organizing data
1-13	The Menu (4-6)	comparing; observing
1-14	The Art of French Cooking (4-6)	collecting and organizing data; classifying
1-15	If Only Tables Could Talk (4-6)	imagining
1-16	Cooking with Chef Jacques (4-6)	observing
1-17	The Countdown (4-6)	classifying; criticizing
1-18	We're Open! (4-6)	observing; criticizing

Black American History

1-19	Afro Game (4-6)	looking for assumptions; collecting and organizing data; interpreting

ACTIVITY TITLE AND GRADE LEVEL	SKILLS USED

Imagination Games

1-20	Oranges Everywhere (K-3)	imagining
1-21	Orange Essence (K-3)	imagining
1-22	Adjectives About (K-3)	imagining
1-23	What If? (K-3)	imagining

Topics for Further Study

Bibliography

It's Me, Only Me!

The following four activities are designed to improve self-concept and create an awareness of how we are alike and yet uniquely different. There is opportunity to work successfully individually and as a part of a group.

1-1 LIKES AND DISLIKES (K-3)

Objective: After completing this activity, the student should be able to relate personal preferences and activities to his or her body.

Materials Needed:

- drawing paper
- glue
- pencils or crayons
- old magazines
- scissors

Procedure:

1. Have the students draw a person's shape as large as the paper will allow. (You can use butcher paper and draw a life-sized shape, but this does take more time for the students to complete.) Tell the students that this will be their own personal self.

2. Have the students look through the magazines for things they like to see, hear, smell, taste, and think about or do. The pictures of things they think about are to be cut out and glued on the drawn head. The other pictures can be placed on different parts of the body. The trunk and limbs of the drawing

might be where the students glue those pictures of things that require physical activity, or use of their arms and legs, or for how their body must move.

3. After each personal self is finished, have the students organize themselves into different groups such as: those students who like to eat tomatoes, those students who like to run barefoot on the beach, or those students who like to see movies.

4. Ask the students to tell you things they observed in these groups. What was the most unique thing they saw? Were there many groups? What did they discover about themselves and the other students?

5. You may want to place the drawings on the wall as a bulletin board. Invite the students to make up questions and add to the display such things as: "What two students like to eat spinach?" "Which 23 'selves' like pizza?" "Which student likes to have his hair cut?"

1-2 MOTTO ME (K-3)

Objective: After completing this activity, the student should be able to invent an imaginative saying about him- or herself.

Materials Needed:

- paper
- pencil

- scraps of construction paper

Procedure:

1. Tell the students they are going to be inventors. They work in the Motto Lab Company and their clients want them to come up with unique sayings about themselves. The clients hope that the sayings will lead to further publication. Explain that as the Motto Lab Company is in the business of publishing and inventing famous mottos, it would be a real feather in their cap to land this contract!

2. You may want to say some well-known and not-so-well-known sayings to give your students an idea. Some suggestions are:

"I will...because I can!"

"Mistakes are simply invitations to try again."

"My attitude determines my altitude."

"Your day goes the way the corners of your mouth turn."

3. After the students have written their mottos, let them use scrap paper to decorate the sayings.

1-3 ALL RIGHT! (K-3)

Objective: After completing this activity, the student should be able to design motto cards that share a feeling.

Materials Needed:

- magazines
- scissors
- construction paper
- fine-tipped markers
- glue

Procedure:

1. Tell the students that they have really outdone themselves! Their mottos have impressed the clients and a contract has been given to publish them as a series of greeting or motto cards. So the students have to get started on developing them.
2. Divide the class into appropriate groups to design a series of ten cards based on a theme, such as friendship, love, getting along with others, feeling good about oneself, or happy thoughts. Perhaps some students will want to design their own box of ten assorted themes.
3. Have the students use the magazines to find ideas on themes from the ads. These pictures can then be cut out and glued to the homemade greeting cards.
4. Expand this activity as far as your students want to take it. You might, for example, have the cards printed by your school's printing department or by a commercial printing company. These cards can then be sold as a fund raiser. Or take appropriate cards to a local nursing home, send them to friends, or mail them to pen pals in different cities.
5. Remind the students that since they're an expanding company, they might want to come up with a company logo—or even a new name for the company.

1-4 WOW, ARE YOU SURE? (K-3)

Objective: After completing this activity, the student should be able to assist in creating a melody that shares a feeling.

Materials Needed: none

Procedure:

1. Tell the students that a music store just overheard their tremendous success in the card publishing business. The Overhear Music Company now wants them to create a song, not just any song, but a song that will help change sad feelings into happy ones.

2. Brainstorm with your students all of the words associated with happy feelings, such as yellow balloons, smiling faces, a frisky puppy. Accept all of the suggestions without comment and enjoy writing them all over the chalkboard!

3. Now divide your class into groups of two to three members each. Challenge the students to think of a time when they felt sad. What made them feel better?

4. Have each group try to come up with a few lines of the song that will change a sad feeling into a happy one. (You might want to write the words that the younger students come up with.) The students may use a melody they already know, but encourage them to be creative and think of new melodies.

5. Let each group sing its song after everyone has finished with the words. A student or two might even want to accompany the groups with an instrument.

The following three activities help students develop their communication and decision-making skills. Students will gain many insights into their own unique qualities.

1-5 OFF TO THE STARS (K-3)

Objective: After completing this activity, the student will be able to state several of his or her own special and unique qualities.

Materials Needed:

- copies of the "My Star" sheets
- pencils

Procedure:

1. Hand out stars and ask students to complete the sentences.
2. When everyone has finished ask students to pick a partner. Now it's time to share their stars. Direct the students to share their written responses with each other.

MY STAR

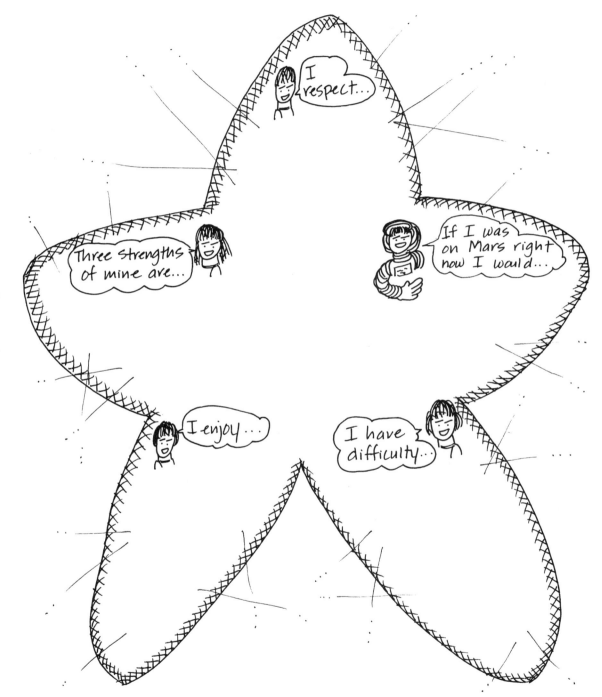

1-6 STARSHARE (K-3)

Objective: After completing this activity the student will be able to share certain special and unique qualities of another student.

Materials Needed:

- completed "My Star" sheets

Procedure:

1. Ask partners to find one other partnership.
2. Share your partner's star "points" with the new partnership. Ample time should be allowed so that each student's star "points" are shared by their partner. This activity helps develop listening skills.

1-7 STARPOWER (K-3)

Objective: After completing this activity the student will be able to tell how it feels to be a part of a group problem-solving effort.

Materials Needed: none

Procedure:

1. Tell the students that they will now have a chance to visually and physically create a machine using only their bodies and voices. The machine should demonstrate how the group of four students plans to work together. It should also demonstrate the important qualities of the team of four.
2. After each team has shared their machine, allow time for discussion. How did it feel to work together as a team? Did anyone in your group try to take charge or was leadership shared by all?

The French Café

The French Café was specifically designed for a French class; however, this line of study can be adapted to encompass other languages and their customs as well as regional customs. This skeleton can be a foundation for creative educators to expand upon, even to explore the possibilities of an alien culture.

1-8 WHAT'S IT ALL ABOUT (4-6)

Objective: After completing this activity the student should be able to describe the various characteristics of a French café.

Materials Needed:

- pictures of a French café
- books or magazines that would describe a café's atmosphere
- a typical menu
- any other books, films, or materials that would inspire the students to create their own café

Procedure:

1. Tell the children that they are going to create and build their own outdoor French café.
2. They may begin brainstorming ideas stimulated by the materials and discussions provided by the teacher and classmates. Examples of topics that can be discussed are: music, food, drink, atmosphere, and the most important purpose of the café (to meet friends).
3. To further stimulate motivation and creative thinking you may choose to take the children on an imaginary journey. So...put on your walking shoes and beret and drink in the sights and sounds of Paris.

Example:

As we tiptoe from canvas to canvas, we see budding artists capturing the famous Byzantine-style basilica, Sacre Coeur, in Monmartre. They paint in the style of their favorite artists whose masterpieces hang in the Louvre. As we travel along Avenue de L'Opera toward the Louvre, we stop in front of the Place de L'Opera. If we listen carefully, we can hear melodies floating through the very cracks of the building. (At this time, you may want to play a few pieces from specific works: Saint-Säens' "Carnival of the Animals" and "Danse Macabre" or Jacques Offenbach's "Can-Can" from *Orpheus in Hades.)* As we hum the "Can-Can," we approach the grand entrance of the "Golden Prison," the Louvre. Inside, we're amazed to see how small Leonardo da Vinci's "Mona Lisa" is, the simplicity of Degas' café in "Glass of Absinthe," and the beautifully blended colors in Renoir's masterpiece "Le Moulin de la Galette." Continuing our journey, we cross the Seine to Notre Dame and its famed flying buttresses. The silence is suddenly broken as the bells toll. Could it be Victor Hugo's Hunchback of Notre Dame, Quasimodo?! With our ears still ringing we walk down the left bank, again crossing the Seine, and continue past a beautiful garden, Jardin des Tuileries. We stop and take time, as the Parisiennes do, to take in the beauty around us. After our long day we have become quite hungry and thirsty. We finally stop at a café on the Champs Elysees that has a beautiful view of the Arc de Triomphe. We order the simple café food and drink, discuss the adventures of our day, and just drink in the sights and sounds around us. (You may choose to serve grape juice and French bread to the children.)

1-9 SURVEYING THE SITUATION (4-6)

Objective: After completing this activity the student should be able to determine an appropriate location for their outdoor café.

Materials Needed:

- tape measure or yardstick
- pencil
- paper
- large piece of paper for blueprint
- magic markers

Procedure:

1. Now the class is actually ready to decide on their location.
2. Have the class survey the grounds of the school and determine the best-suited spot to build their outdoor café. Remind the children that they are looking for an area with natural beauty, shaded areas, flowering surroundings, open space for the tables, and availability to a cooking area.
3. When the location is agreed upon, have the children take measurements of the area and make notes of the natural and man-made surroundings. When the children return to the classroom, they can make a landscape blueprint of the location.
4. After the landscape blueprint has been drawn, the children can add their exterior boundaries and interior furnishings of the café. Now we're really rolling!

1-10 SETTING THE SCENE (4-6)

Objective: After completing this activity the student should be able to name many of the typical outdoor scenes found at a French sidewalk café.

Materials Needed:

- paint
- paint brushes
- mural paper

- newspaper
- stakes
- tape

Procedure:

1. In order to create the exterior structure the children will need to paint murals. These murals will become the walls and boundaries of the café. Tell the children to imagine they are sitting in a French café and have them recreate their visual images. Here are a few examples you may want to suggest:

    —**people walking on the sidewalk past the café**

    —**a beautiful view of the fountain in the park**

    —**the Eiffel Tower in the distance**

    —**the flowerwomen selling their beautiful flowers**

    —**waiters waiting on other tables**

    —**someone sitting at the bar**

2. Stakes can be used to secure the murals when they are ready to be erected.

1-11 NOW, SET THE MOOD (4-6)

Objective: After completing this activity the student should be able to identify and select various French music pieces that they can use for their café.

Materials Needed:

- varied selections of French music

- tape recorder or record player

Procedure:

1. No restaurant, American or French, is complete without music. Can't you picture yourself nibbling on some brie, sipping on sparkling grape juice, while listening to Chopin? While the children are working on their other activities, you can play the music and have them select pieces for the café. The children will enjoy listening to classical pieces as well as pop vocalists.

2. At this time, committees can be formed and final activities can be completed by the members of each committee.

1-12 SPREAD THE WORD (4-6)

Objective: After this activity the student should be able to identify several ways to advertise the opening of their café. The student will be able to point out key phrases that would describe their café.

Materials Needed:

- newspaper
- magic markers
- poster board
- pencils
- tape

Procedure:

1. You need to spread the word. The adult population at your school needs to know the date, location, and the hours the café will be open. Let the students know that it "pays to advertise."

2. Have the children look through newspapers and locate advertisements for theater productions and special community events. Point out the abbreviated writing style, creativity, and clarity of these messages. Have the committee create several posters "spreading the word." These signs can be posted throughout the school. The advertising committee also needs to create a "logo" for the café.

3. If you have access to a VCR, your marketing staff can write and film a commercial which can be shown to the entire school.

1-13 THE MENU (4-6)

Objective: After this activity the student should be able to draw a picture that reflects some of the style of French impressionistic painters.

Materials Needed:

- examples of menus from different restaurants
- paper
- pencils
- water color paints
- paint brushes
- copies or pictures of French impressionistic works

Procedure:

1. Tell the menu committee they will be designing the entire menu from cover to content. Among the many talents the French possess, they are famous for their artwork.

2. Take time to view some French paintings. Have the children compare their styles to that of other painters, such as Picasso or Van Gogh.

3. In keeping with Monet and Renoir's style, the children will paint a master-piece on the cover of each menu.

1-14 THE ART OF FRENCH COOKING (4-6)

Objective: After completing this activity the student will be able to identify several French desserts that they will use at the café.

Materials Needed:

- French cookbooks
- French cooking magazines with color photos
- pencils
- paper

Procedure:

1. Most children have not sampled exquisite French cuisine. Not only will the children taste fine French cooking, they will become the master chefs. After researching several cookbooks, have the children choose three desserts that will be easy to prepare, can be made in advance, and can be obtained at a moderate cost. If time or convenience is a factor, other items can be substituted for or accompany the desserts.

Examples:

Crepes avec la Glace et Chocolat Sauce (ice cream-filled crepe with chocolate sauce)

Cremeuse Bouffee (cream puff)

Creme Fraiche Fruits (fruit topped with fresh cream)

Biscuits au Chocolat (sponge cakes with chocolate)

Petits Fours (sponge cakes)

Peches Cardinal avec Creme Chantilly (peach halves smothered in raspberry sauce with whipped cream)

Compote de Fruits (fruit poached in vanilla syrup)

Mousse au Chocolat (chocolate mousse)

Creme Caramel (caramel custard)

Tartes aux Fraises (fresh strawberry tarts)

Les Crudites (raw vegetables with homemade dip)

Omelette (French omelet)

Quiche au Fromage (open-face cheese tart)

Cheeses: Camembert, Port-Salut, Cantal, Brie, Munster

Fruits: grapes, pears, apples, etc.

2. Also, have the children add to their grocery list: loaves of French bread, fruit, and cheese for each table. But of course...don't forget the sparkling grape juice!

1-15 IF ONLY TABLES COULD TALK (4-6)

Objective: After completing this activity the student should be able to describe a historic French character in a fictional format. The student will recognize that the French franc is similar to the U.S. dollar.

Materials Needed:

- pencils
- paper
- imagination

Procedure:

1. The many legends and stories that were told in the French cafés still live in memory among the old tables and worn walls. Perhaps some famous writer—Moliere, Dumas, Voltaire; painters—Renoir, Degas, Cezanne; or musicians—Berlioz, Debussy, or Ravel, frequented your café in his day. Tell the children they are going to add character to their café by giving it a history. Have the committee write a creative story and attach it to the inside cover of the menu.

2. Providing the children with an understanding of the French monetary system will help them establish prices for their food items as well as convert their prices to the American dollar. The French franc is similar to the American dollar in that 100 centimes equals one franc as 100 pennies equals one dollar. The exchange rate changes frequently; however, leading banks can provide you with up-to-date figures. At this time, the dollar is worth approximately eight francs. In the French café, usually desserts, fruits, cheeses, and breads are under two dollars or 16 francs.

3. After the desserts have been chosen and priced, the children may add them to the menu. Also, a description in English will accompany each dessert. The children will decide on the prices and convert them into francs; however, American coins will be accepted. You may also want the children to include food items that are compliments of the house: sparkling grape juice, breads, cheeses, and fruits.

1-16 COOKING WITH CHEF JACQUES (4-6)

Objective: After completing this activity the student will be able to demonstrate how to make various French desserts.

Materials Needed:

- individual recipe ingredients
- cooking facilities
- utensils

Procedure:

1. Your opening day will run much more smoothly if an abundance of the food is prepared ahead of time.
2. the children will only have to dip, slice, arrange, and serve during the opening day "rush hour." All the children will have the experience of cooking and the delight of making the desserts look elegant!

1-17 THE COUNTDOWN (4-6)

Objective: After completing this activity the student should be able to understand the use of a "check-off list."

Materials Needed:

- food items
- checkoff list
- furnishings for café
- children
- all odds and ends for café

Procedure:

1. The opening day of the café will be extremely busy.
2. Each child should know his/her responsibilities to ensure that all areas will be covered. Below is a helpful check-off list:

_____ Are the murals up and secured?

_____ Is the cashier's stand filled with coins and ready for operation?

_____ Are the tables and chairs properly placed?

_____ Are the tables covered with tablecloths or white paper?

_____ Are there baskets of cheese, fruit, and bread on each table?

_____ Are there wine glasses set at each place?

_____ Do you have enough paper plates, napkins, forks, or spoons?

_____ Do you have everything that you may need out of the freezer?

_____ Does each child have a writing pad and pencil?

_____ Do you have extension cords, if needed, for the music?

_____ Is there a table provided for dirty dishes, etc.?

1-18 WE'RE OPEN! (4-6)

Objective: After completing this activity the student should be able to express the various job responsibilities necessary in the café.

Materials Needed:

- customers!!!

Procedure:

1. The children will be waiting excitedly at their places. The kitchen staff will be ready for incoming orders. The maitre d' will seat the customers while the waiters and waitresses busily begin taking orders.
2. The boys, in their black pants, white shirts, and red bow ties, will look very French pouring sparkling grape juice while a white towel hangs from their arm. The girls, with their dark skirts, white shirts, and frilly aprons will seem so authentic as they greet their customers in their native tongue...French. While the French music plays in the background, you will hear sighs of contentment, see happy faces, and know it all went well.
3. Halfway through, the children will switch jobs so they may experience all types of jobs.
4. Most of the food can be donated by parents.
5. Profits can go to the school library to buy additional French materials.

Black American History

1-19 AFRO GAME (4-6)

Objective: After completing this activity the student should be able to remember the names and contributions of certain blacks to American history.

Materials Needed:

- copies of the AFRO playing cards
- cover chips (laminated squares)
- copies of "Black Contributions and Achievements in America" sheets

Procedure:

AFRO is a bingo-type game which students will enjoy playing. To play it effectively, however, this game should include the following steps:

1. Make AFRO cards and cover chips. The cards should be cut out, mounted on posterboard, and laminated. An easy way to make the chips is to laminate posterboard first and then cut it into small squares. However, any type of chips or markers can be used. Add the names of local and state black leaders in the blank spaces on the AFRO cards.

2. Give students study sheets to do research on items 1–51 of the "Black Contributions and Achievements in America" sheets. Research may be done by pairs of students.

3. After ample research time, have a class discussion on their findings, making sure each child has all correct answers to study before playing AFRO. Make certain that the facts come to life by associating a picture of the famous person *with* his/her accomplishments or by including special details and human interest information.

4. Give out AFRO cards and cover chips. (NOTE: Give students the option of either playing with a partner or alone.)

5. You (the teacher) are the caller. Read clues from answer sheet in "first person singular." (*Example:* "I escaped from slavery in 1849 and later led more than 300 slaves to freedom—Who am I?") Using a pencil, lightly check off each name from your caller sheet. When you hear a student call out "AFRO!" silently check student's game card against your caller sheet. If student is incorrect, do not tell him/her which one is incorrect, but rather continue playing the game until someone correctly gets AFRO (BINGO).

6. You are encouraged to incorporate local black leaders into bingo game cards in "open spaces."

Options:

Play "Black Out" by having each student attempt to cover his/her entire card, four corners, inside square, etc.

"Afro Game" Answers

1. Harriet Tubman
2. Muhammad Ali
3. Alex Haley
4. Hank Aaron
5. Shirley Chisholm
6. Edward Brooke
7. Pedro Alonzo Nina
8. Benjamin Banneker
9. Garrett Morgan
10. Matthew Henson
11. Dr. Daniel Williams
12. Crispus Attucks
13. Martin Luther King, Jr.
14. Jim Brown
15. Elizabeth D. Koonce
16. George Washington Carver
17. Mary McLeod Bethune
18. Jackie Robinson
19. Langston Hughes
20. Althea Gibson
21. John H. Johnson
22. Peter Salem & Salem Poor
23. Sidney Poitier
24. James Gardiner & James Miles
25. Dorie Miller
26. Frederick Davison
27. William Thompson
28. Nat Turner
29. Rosa Parks
30. Thurgood Marshall
31. Booker T. Washington
32. Phillis Wheatley
33. Charles Drew
34. W.C. Handy
35. Jan Matzeliger
36. Madame C.J. Walker
37. Marian Anderson
38. Diana Ross
39. W.E.B. Du Bois
40. Kareem Abdul-Jabbar
41. Malcolm X
42. Jack Johnson
43. Frederick Douglass
44. Marva Collins
45. Carter G. Woodson
46. James Weldon Johnson
47. James Earl Jones
48. Lorraine Hansberry
49. Tom Bradley
50. Guy Blufford, Jr.
51. Vanessa Williams

1.

AFRO

A	F	R	O	
CARTER G. WOODSON	CRISPUS ATTUCKS	JAN MATZELIGER	MALCOLM X	GARRETT MORGAN
	MARY McLEOD BETHUNE	W.E.B. DuBOIS	ELIZABETH D. KOONCE	
MARTIN LUTHER KING, JR.	FREDERICK DOUGLASS	FREE SPACE	JACK JOHNSON	
SIDNEY POITIER	EDWARD BROOKE	ROSA PARKS	MARIAN ANDERSON	MARVA COLLINS
JOHN H. JOHNSON	DORIE MILLER	BENJAMIN BANNEKER	CHARLES DREW	KAREEM ABDUL-JABBAR

2.

AFRO

A	F	R	O	
CARTER G. WOODSON	JACK JOHNSON	FREDERICK DOUGLASS	BOOKER T. WASHINGTON	TOM BRADLEY
JAMES WELDON JOHNSON	FREDERICK DAVISON	JAMES EARL JONES	LORRAINE HANSBERRY	
MATTHEW HENSON	PEDRO ALONZA NINA	FREE SPACE	SHIRLEY CHISHOLM	HANK AARON
JACKIE ROBINSON	JAN MATZELIGER	GARRETT MORGAN	CRISPUS ATTUCKS	
HARRIET TUBMAN	DIANA ROSS	W.E.B. DuBOIS	MARIAN ANDERSON	MARVA COLLINS

3.

AFRO

A	F	R	O	
JAN MAT-ZELIGER	PEDRO ALONZA NINA	HANK AARON	ALEX HALEY	MUHAMMAD ALI
BENJAMIN BANNEKER	EDWARD BROOKE	SHIRLEY CHISHOLM	NAT TURNER	
	TOM BRADLEY	FREE SPACE	GARRETT MORGAN	JIM BROWN
FREDERICK DOUGLASS	MARVA COLLINS	CARTER G. WOODSON	MATTHEW HENSON	DORIE MILLER
MALCOLM X	ALTHEA GIBSON	SIDNEY POITIER		ALEX HALEY

4.

AFRO

A	F	R	O	
JAN MAT-ZELIGER	ALEX HALEY	MADAME C.J. WALKER	KAREEM ABDUL-JABBAR	MALCOLM X
WILLIAM THOMPSON	MARIAN ANDERSON	DIANA ROSS	THURGOOD MARSHALL	NAT TURNER
ELIZABETH COFIELD	DORIE MILLER	FREE SPACE	ROSA PARKS	JAMES GARDINER
CHARLES DREW	SALEM POOR	LANGSTON HUGHES	PHILLIS WHEATLEY	HANK AARON
CRISPUS ATTUCKS	DANIEL HALE WILLIAMS	MARVA COLLINS	MUHAMMAD ALI	JACK JOHNSON

AFRO

		FREE SPACE		

AFRO

		FREE SPACE		

Black Contributions and Achievements in America

1. _____ escaped from slavery in 1849. Later, she led more than 300 slaves to freedom.

2. _____ became World Heavyweight Champion for the second time in 1974.

3. *Roots,* a book by _____, told the story of the author's family from its origins in Africa, making both Blacks and Whites more aware of Black American History.

4. _____ broke Babe Ruth's all-time home run record in 1974.

5. _____ of New York became the first Black woman to serve in the United States Congress and campaigned for, but did not win, the 1972 Democratic Presidential nomination.

6. _____ of Massachusetts became the first Black United States Senator since Reconstruction.

7. _____ was the navigator of one of Columbus' ships, the *Nina.*

8. _____ constructed one of the first clocks in America; he was also appointed by President George Washington to lay out the boundaries for the District of Columbia.

9. _____ found a way to help people to be safe by constructing the first traffic light.

10. _____ was the only American who accompanied Robert Peary when the explorer reached the North Pole in 1909.

11. _____ performed the first successful open-heart surgery.

12. _____ was the first Black to be killed by British Red Coats in the Boston Massacre in a fight for American Independence (The American Revolutionary War).

13. _____ was leader of the Montgomery, Alabama bus boycott, which started the nonviolence fight for the Civil Rights Act.

14. _____ was a football player who retired to become an actor. He set records for more yards gained than any other player in the National Football League history.

15. _____ was the first Black woman to serve as President of the National Education Association (NEA) in 1968.

16. _____ was a famous scientist who made more than 300 products from the peanut, 118 products from the sweet potato, and 75 products from the pecan.

17. With only $1.50 and five students, _____ opened a college in Florida to improve the educational opportunities for Blacks.

18. The first to integrate major-league baseball was _____.

19. An outstanding Black poet and short-story writer who expressed despair of Blacks over their social and economic conditions was _____.

20. _____ was the first Black person to play in the Wimbledon Tennis Tournament.

21. _____ is publisher of *Ebony, Jet,* and *Negro Digest.*

22. _____ and _____ were heroes of the Battle of Bunker Hill, 1775.

23. _____ became the first Black to win an "Oscar" as best actor of the year in 1964.

24. Private _____ and Corporal _____ were among 13 Black soldiers to win Medals of Honor in a battle during the Civil War. There were 166 all-Black units in this war.

25. _____ was the first hero of World War II awarded the Navy Cross.

26. The first Black combat general was _____.

27. Private _____ died a hero 10 days before his 23rd birthday in the Korean War.

28. _____ led the slaves of Southhampton County, Virginia, in a revolt against slavery in 1831.

29. _____ refused to give up her bus seat to a White man in Montgomery, Alabama, in 1955. This helped bring about the civil rights movement in the United States.

30. In 1967, _____ became the first Black to be appointed as an associate justice of the United States Supreme Court.

31. _____ established a normal school for Black students that later became Tuskegee Institute in Alabama. He was well-known as a writer and a speaker.

32. _____, a poet, was born in West Africa and was brought to the American colonies as a slave in 1761. She is recognized as the first Black author in the United States.

33. _____ , a surgeon, became known for his research on blood plasma transfusions and for the organization of blood banks.

34. _____, Father of the Blues, is best known as the man who wrote "St. Louis Blues."

35. The first shoemaking machine was invented by _____.

36. One of the first female millionaires was _____, a businesswoman. She invented a new method of straightening hair, a hair softener, and a special straightening comb.

37. _____ was the first Black American woman to sing with the Metropolitan Opera.

38. _____ is a leading popular singer and an actress in motion pictures. Her best-known role was as Billie Holiday in *Lady Sings the Blues*.

39. One of the most important leaders of Black protest in the United States and a founder of the NAACP was _____. Two of his best-known books are *The Souls of Black Folk* and *Black Reconstruction in America*.

40. _____, over seven feet tall, was a basketball star at UCLA during his college career. He then went on to all-pro honors with the Milwaukee Bucks and Los Angeles Lakers.

41. A "Black Nationalist" who believed that Black Americans should form a nation separate from White Americans was _____. He was assassinated in 1965.

42. The first Black American to be World Heavyweight Champion was _____ .

43. _____ was born in slavery and became the greatest of the Black abolitionists before the Civil War.

44. _____ was founder of the Westside Preparatory School in Chicago for underachievers. She started this school in her home with only 9 pupils.

45. Father of Black History is _____.

46. The Black National Anthem, "Lift Ev'ry Voice and Sing," was written by _____, who also wrote numerous books and songs including *God's Trombones* and "The Creation."

47. One of the leading American actors is _____. He played leading roles in Shakespeare's *Othello* and in the play and movie *The Great White Hope*.

48. While still in her 20's, _____ wrote *A Raisin in the Sun,* a play about a Black family in Chicago. She died of cancer at age 34. After her death, a collection of her writings was published as *To Be Young, Gifted and Black.*

49. _____ was elected Mayor of Los Angeles in 1973 and is one of the most respected civic leaders in the United States.

50. _____ became the first Black American to fly into space on August 30, 1983.

51. _____ (Miss New York) became the first Black Miss America on September 17, 1983.

Imaging is the process during which an individual mentally or physically manipulates an image. This unit focuses on teaching the child to deliberately imagine. Piaget believes that as a child matures, spontaneous play decreases and the ability to imagine becomes internalized and exhibited through fantasies and daydreams. The teacher's role is to create a trusting, warm, sensitive environment that encourages expression and thereby far-reaching possibilities in terms of thinking and creativity. The following activities encourage students to utilize imagery as a thinking tool.

1-20 ORANGES EVERYWHERE (K-3)

Objective: After completing this activity the student should be able to visualize an orange in his or her mind's eye.

Materials Needed:

- oranges
- paper

- crayons

Procedure:

1. Begin by introducing the word *imagination*. Break the word into smaller parts; *image* and *imagine*. Discuss these smaller words. In the discussion, direct students to recall various experiences in which they used imaging/imagined/imagination.

2. Now introduce the main activity by passing around oranges and instructing students to utilize all of their senses in exploring the oranges. Inform students that the oranges are going to be the main attraction for a number of activities intended to develop imagery and imagination skills. Brainstorm as a group all of the things noticed as students examine the oranges. Use chart paper for the brainstorm list. (The chart will be used for the next three activities.) Isolate characteristics from the brainstorm list that are visually stimulated. Instruct the students to close their eyes and imagine the oranges visually. Slowly, using a very calm, serious voice, instruct students to imagine two oranges, three oranges, four oranges, a basketful, a wagonful of oranges, and finally a room full of oranges. Have the students hold an image of oranges in their mind. Ask that they place themselves in the room with the oranges. Allow silence for a minute.

3. Now instruct students to open their eyes and draw what their image was at the end of the exercise.

4. Optional: Write a creative story entitled "A Day Full of Oranges."

1-21 ORANGE ESSENCE (K-3)

Objective: After completing this activity the student will be able to utilize their sense of smell in a brainstorming activity.

Materials Needed:

- oranges—one per student
- paper
- crayons
- pencils
- knives

Procedure:

1. Begin by passing out oranges, one per student. Have children reflect on the previous activity with oranges. Review the "brainstorm" list. Inform students that the focus of this session is on the smell of oranges. Before cutting the oranges, instruct students to close their eyes and imagine the room full of oranges. Students are encouraged to add the sense of smell to their mental image. A quiet pause is necessary at this point. Cut the oranges into quarters and have the students smell them. Once again, students close their eyes and hold the mental image of oranges.

2. Brainstorm individually in picture form all of the things that would be better if they smelled like oranges.

1-22 ADJECTIVES ABOUND (K-3)

Objective: After completing this activity the student should be able to use various adjectives to describe an orange.

Materials Needed:

- oranges cut into quarters

Procedure:

1. Reflect on the past two activities. Share the "brainstorm" list from the first activity with oranges. Discuss which characteristics students have not explored (i.e., taste, touch). Pause for a minute to reform a mental image of oranges using visual and olfactory cues.

2. Divide the large group into small groups and distribute oranges. Write the words "Adjectives Abound" on the chalkboard. Ask the students to guess what today's activity is. Review what an adjective is and use examples to check for understanding. Share the rules for "Adjectives Abound" with the groups:

    (a) You must communicate with group members.

    (b) You must speak only in adjectives and nonverbal cues. No sentences or phrases can be used unless totally composed of adjectives.

3. Students should then be instructed to tune into the taste and texture of the oranges as they play "Adjectives Abound."

4. Pull back together as a large group for discussion. Share adjectives used in small groups and compile a master list. Discuss frustrations and feelings. Remind students to focus only on taste and texture. Pause and instruct students to hold a mental image of oranges using several senses.

5. Optional: Brainstorm foods that could have an orange flavor added (e.g., orange chicken, orange chocolate).

1-23 WHAT IF? (K-3)

Objective: After completing this activity the student should be able to relate imagination to stressful problem-solving situations.

Materials Needed:

Procedure:

1. Reflect on past activities. Encourage students to share any experiences that they have had in imaging or daydreaming in the past few weeks.

2. Introduce "What if."

3. Ask students to share uncomfortable or fear-filled experiences (e.g., going to the dentist). Guide students. What if you loved oranges and you were scared of the dentist? What could you do to ease the anxiety and fear?

4. Create a calm, quiet atmosphere and ask students to sit comfortably with closed eyes for the following guided visualization:

> "Imagine that today is the day you are going to the dentist. You hate visiting the dentist. You worried all last night about going today. Now it is time for your appointment. You are with your mother getting on the elevator. She pushes the button for the fifth floor. You wish the elevator would break and not stop on the floor where your dentist has her office. But the elevator doors open and you see your dentist's office doors. All you can think about is running away. As you walk into the waiting room the receptionist smiles. Your stomach feels funny and you feel jittery all over. You sit down with your mother and want to appear brave. You look at a book to relax. Something makes you think of oranges. Wow, do you love oranges! You imagine you have a fresh, plump orange. You feel more relaxed just thinking about having an orange. You imagine peeling the orange. The skin is shiny and smooth. As you peel back the outside of the orange, you see it is very juicy. It smells so good and sweet. How you love the smell of oranges. As you take a bite of your orange, your mouth waters. It is such a juicy orange. You enjoy every bite of the orange. Your mother touches your arm and it's your turn to see the dentist. Somehow, you feel relaxed all over. As you enter the room and sit in the chair you think of the wonderful taste and smell of oranges. You feel calm and relaxed. You are no longer afraid."

5. Discuss with the class their feelings during the guided visualization. Discuss possible applications. Guide students to apply their techniques in stressful problem-solving situations.

RESEARCH TOPICS FOR FURTHER STUDY OF
"DISCOVERING MYSELF AND THE WORLD AROUND ME"

Presented here are a collection of research topics for the inquiring mind. The topics are designed to encourage divergent as well as convergent thinking. *Beware:* young researchers may end up detouring into uncharted waters of knowledge and discovery. The teacher/facilitator should encourage and welcome these departures.

1. Design a family journal which includes interviews with each member of your family. Tape record the interviews first.
2. Develop a written family portrait which describes the characteristics, careers, and recreations of your ancestors.
3. Create a model which depicts your family. Include a written description of why you chose certain materials for the construction of the model.
4. Develop a journal which describes your neighborhood. Include data on when and from where the families emigrated.
5. Imagine yourself as an animal (other than human). What type of an animal would you be and why?
6. Imagine yourself 10 years from now. How about 20 years? 30? Draw a self-portrait at each of these stages.
7. Analyze the different roles you have. How do you act in school? How about at home? Does it change when you are with your friends? How about when you are amongst strangers? Compare and contrast.

BIBLIOGRAPHY FOR
"DISCOVERING MYSELF AND THE WORLD AROUND ME"

About Black America, Activity Book #2420 (Compton, CA: Educational Insights, 1977).

French Government Tourist Office, Suite 1702, 111 N. Washington Avenue, Chicago, IL 60602. Posters and brochures.

Multicultural Spoken Here by Josephine Chase and Linda Parth (Santa Monica, CA: Goodyear Publishing Company, 1982). Discovering America's people through language arts and library skills.

Self-Concept and School Achievement by William Purkey (Englewood Cliffs, NJ: Prentice-Hall, 1970).

Teaching the Black Experience: Methods and Materials by James A. Banks (Belmont, CA: Fearon Publishers, 1970).

Section 2

MATH AMAZING

The activities that follow will set the stage for students wishing to explore the horizons of the math world. Young mathematicians will voyage through the worlds of architecture, consumerism, banking, and metrics as they acquire many new skills. Perhaps they will participate in a Math Week or design and test a load-bearing structure. The possibilities, as you will discover, are infinite.

ACTIVITY TITLE AND GRADE LEVEL	SKILLS USED
Budgeting and Banking	
2-1 Money Talks (4-6)	problem solving; comparing; organizing data
2-2 Budgeting (4-6)	problem solving; organizing data
Take Me to Your Liter, 'Cause I Want to Meter	
2-3 The History of Metrics (4-6)	collecting data
2-4 Metric Map (4-6)	collecting and organizing data
2-5 Metric Scavenger Hunt (4-6)	collecting and organizing data
2-6 I Want to Meter (4-6)	comparing; coding
2-7 Decimeter Jump (K-3)	observing; comparing
2-8 Metric Measuring Mania (4-6)	observing; comparing; collecting and organizing data

ACTIVITY TITLE AND GRADE LEVEL	SKILLS USED
2-9 Residential Design (4-6)	observing; collecting and organizing data

Consumer Math

2-10 Food Forum (4-6)	imagining; classifying
2-11 Fruit Search (4-6)	observing; collecting and organizing data; problem solving
2-12 Ad Vantage (4-6)	collecting and organizing data; comparing; interpreting
2-13 Goods and Services (4-6)	problem solving; interpreting; coding; summarizing
2-14 Let's Eat Out! (4-6)	coding; looking for assumptions; interpreting
2-15 What's In It! (4-6)	collecting and organizing data; looking for assumptions

Environmental Geometry

2-16 Shapes Alive Braindrawing (K-3)	observing
2-17 Shape Scientists (K-3)	collecting and organizing data
2-18 Outdoor Wonderland (K-3)	collecting and organizing data
2-19 Shape Artistry (K-3)	coding

ACTIVITY TITLE AND GRADE LEVEL   SKILLS USED

2-20	Geometric Recursion (K-3)	observing; collecting and organizing data, coding; problem solving
2-21	Shapes Recipes (K-3)	imagining
2-22	Sharing Recipes (K-3)	interpreting; problem solving
2-23	Repeating Patterns Collage (K-3)	observing; classifying
2-24	Shapes Movements (K-3)	coding; imagining; problem solving
2-25	Fractals (K-3)	observing; coding; classifying
2-26	Playground Geometry I (K-3)	imagining; problem solving
2-27	Playground Geometry II (K-3)	hypothesis; imagining; problem solving

Numeralonics

2-28	Make a Logo (K-3)	imagining; problem solving
2-29	Logo Rodeo (K-3)	comparing; criticizing
2-30	The Nature of Number/Numeral (K-3)	compare and contrast
2-31	Numeral Time Machine (K-3)	observing; comparing; imagining; interpreting

ACTIVITY TITLE AND GRADE LEVEL	SKILLS USED
2-31 Numeral Time Machine (K-3)	observing; comparing; imagining; interpreting
2-32 I Got the System (K-3)	problem solving
Math Happenings	
2-33 Measurement Monday (K-3)	observing; comparing; collecting and organizing data
2-34 Student Teaching Tuesday (K-3)	interpreting; problem solving
2-35 Workers' Wednesday (K-3)	interpreting
2-36 Try to Guess Thursday (K-3)	observing; hypothesizing
2-37 Far Away Friday (K-3)	imagining; collecting and organizing data
2-38 Math-Go-Round (K-3)	interpreting; collecting and organizing data
Calculator Chatter	
2-39 Babbles (4-6)	collecting and organizing data; problem solving
Architecture Around Us	
2-40 What's Happening Here? (K-3)	observing; coding
2-41 Pulling Apart an Idea (K-3)	comparing; observing

ACTIVITY TITLE AND GRADE LEVEL   SKILLS USED

2-42   Chairperson (K-3)   observing; imagining;
                                            hypothesizing

2-43   By Way of the Bridge (K-3)   observing; comparing; coding;
                                            interpreting; problem solving

2-44   Load It On...1 (K-3)   observing; interpreting

2-45   Load It On...2 (K-3)   predicting; observing;
                                            hypothesis; collecting data;
                                            interpreting

2-46   Load It On...3 (K-3)   comparing; summarizing;
                                            problem solving; collecting
                                            and organizing data;
                                            interpreting

Research Topics for Further Study

Bibliography

Budgeting and Banking

This unit is a practical way to teach both math and grammar application and money management in real-life situations. It is an excellent motivational tool in that students receive dollar amounts on their papers rather than grades.

2-1 MONEY TALKS (4-6)

Objective: After completing this activity, the student should be able to use and balance a personal checking account.

Materials Needed:

- construction paper checkbook covers
- teacher-made checks
- teacher-made balance sheets
- copies of award certificate

Procedure:

1. Design checks and have a good supply mimeographed. (See the sample check shown here.) Each child needs a checkbook made from construction paper. Give each child his or her first five checks. When the initial five have been used, students must buy additional ones from you (the bank).

No._____	No._____
Date:_____	**G and T BANK**
To:_____	
For:_____	_____ 19_____
Balance _____	PAY TO:_____
Deposit +_____	THE AMOUNT OF $_____
TOTAL ____	_____ Dollars
This Check −	
BALANCE	For:_____ _____

2. Give each child a balance sheet (see the sample shown here) to be used as a check register. He or she must always use a pen and sign his or her name on the balance sheet as it will appear on all checks written.

				's BALANCE SHEET
DATE	CHECK #	DEPOSITS	WITHDRAWALS	BALANCE

3. Start each child's bank account by giving him or her a small amount of money ($5.00) to record on his or her balance sheet and on his or her checkbook stub.

> Students will be able to earn additional money through:
>
> > quality of assignments completed
> >
> > good behavior
> >
> > good banking (balanced checkbooks).
>
> Money may be spent to pay for:
>
> > weekly desk rental
> >
> > incomplete assignments
> >
> > forgetting school materials
> >
> > and getting an "NA" check (Not Accepted).

4. Guide students in setting up banking rules and procedures. That is, the charge for weekly desk rental, checks, lost checkbooks, NA checks, etc.
5. Introduce banking terminology (balance, deposits, withdrawals, overdrawn) to students.
6. Pass out the individual checkbooks and balance sheets and have students deposit their first $5.00 in their accounts. Demonstrate how to write a check. Have students write one for the rent on their desk.
7. Discuss possible problems of having a checking account:

> > overdrawing
> >
> > forgeries
> >
> > loss of checkbooks

8. Discuss with students the cost of a NA check (Not Accepted) and possible ways of getting one:

> > change of signature
> >
> > grammatical errors including spelling
> >
> > incomplete check or stub
> >
> > failure to use a pen
> >
> > erasures or "write-overs"
> >
> > insufficient funds

9. Allow a time for students to make all transactions:

   making deposits

   check-writing

   balancing checkbook with balance sheet

10. The bank (the teacher) must develop and maintain a management system. It is a good idea to put a mark on each correct check and show that it has cleared the bank by placing a X next to the amount on the student's balance sheet.

11. Earning money becomes a challenge if this unit is ended every six to nine weeks and the student with the highest balance is awarded a certificate. Or, award certificates to all students who achieve a certain level of savings.

CERTIFICATE

?Math FIRST Federal?

Congratulations to _____

for maintaining a "high interest" classroom
bank account !! $ $ $

TOTAL : $ _____

• SCHOOL •　　TEACHER

C. Notes
Treasurer

2-2 BUDGETING (4-6)

Objective: After completing this activity, the student should be able to organize a "balanced budget."

Materials Needed:

- teacher-made ledger sheet
- pencils and pens
- teacher-made activity sheets
- task cards

Procedure:

1. Assign each classroom activity a money value in lieu of grades as students complete and deposit in their account.
2. Discuss banking and budgeting vocabulary:

Banking Vocabulary	*Budgeting Vocabulary*
check stub	budget
check register	gross income
deposit	net income
withdrawal	income tax
debit	expenditures
balance	fixed expenses
transaction	ledger
void	consumer
bank statement	impulse buying

3. Have students keep a weekly budget of their *real* income over a period of time. Give students who do not receive an income an imaginary weekly income. This budget might include:

MY INCOME:

Allowances: _____

Earnings: _____

Other: _____

TOTAL INCOME: _____

MY MONEY USES:

Savings: _____

Sharing (list): _____

Spending (list): _____

TOTAL MONEY FOR USES: _____

4. Design a ledger sheet on which students can transfer their weekly income and expenditures.
5. Students can also work with a yearly budget. You might, for example, give students the following table.

   Students are to subtract to find the differences between the income and expenses. The money left each month is put into savings on the chart.

Yearly Budget Sheet

Month	INCOME			Itemized Expenditures		Savings
	Allowances	Earnings	TOTAL	Amount	For (list):	
Jan.	$	$	$	$		$
Feb.						
Mar.						
Apr.						
May						
June						
July						
Aug.						
Sept.						
Oct.						
Nov.						
Dec.						
YEARLY TOTALS	$	$	$	$		$

6. Have the students plot the information from step 5 onto a graph.

7. Let the students design a similar activity sheet where students are given a monthly budget to figure in six months, in one year, and so on.

8. Introduce percents and how to convert percents to decimals. Design several activity sheets on which students can apply this skill.

9. Have the class design task cards from local catalogs and newspapers with percent discounts and have students figure sale prices, taxes, and total prices. This activity has endless possibilities.

10. Students can also be given an imaginary net income of $1,500 to plan a written budget for a family of four. Discuss possible *fixed expenses* as well as *day-to-day expenses.*

11. Students can also do individual budgeting. Give students their hourly wage and have them figure:

> gross weekly income
>
> net income (80% of gross)
>
> income taxes
>
> monthly gross income
>
> and monthly net income.

Students are to plan their monthly budgets accordingly.

Take Me to Your Liter 'Cause I Want to Meter

This unit examines the world of metric measurement and will open new avenues for learning and mathematical investigation. Enjoy!

2-3 THE HISTORY OF METRIC (4-6)

Objective: After completing this project the student should be able to describe the origins of the metric system of measurement.

Materials Needed: none

Procedure:

The metric system of measurement is based on the distance from the North Pole to the Equator. This distance is ten million meters. Ask students to independently research how the metric system of measurement came into being. Share and discuss.

2-4 METRIC MAP (4-6)

Objective: After completing this activity the student should be able to describe where the non-metric countries are located.

Materials Needed:

- outline of a world map for each student
- two crayons
- world geographic maps
- dictionaries

Procedure:

1. If the research into the history of metrics was thorough, students should now know that only Burma, Liberia, Muscat, Southern Yemen, and the United States are non-metric. Ask students to pair up and study the world maps.

2. Find where the non-metric countries are on the world maps. Color the corresponding areas on the personal maps in one color.

3. The rest of the world should be colored in another tint. Each student now has a metric map.

2-5 METRIC SCAVENGER HUNT (4-6)

Objective: After completing this activity the student should be able to identify products in their home which come from metric and non-metric countries.

Materials Needed:

- copies of "Metric Scavenger Hunt" sheet
- completed metric maps from previous activity

Procedure:

1. Review the metric maps. Any product made by a country shaded in the metric color will manufacture products which use metric measurement.

2. Ask each student to first list ten products which are in their homes (e.g., clocks, chairs, foodstuffs, appliances).

3. Once ten items are listed, search the item for identification. Where was it made? List its origin beside the name of the product. A list might look like this:

Item	Origin
1. Clock	Germany
2. Chairs	North Carolina
3. Teapot	Taiwan
4. Truck	U.S.
5. Car	Japan
6. Light fixture	U.S.
7. Cereal box	U.S.
8. Shirt	U.S.
9. Silverware	Germany
10. Vase	Italy

4. Share and discuss results.

METRIC SCAVENGER HUNT

Name _____

Date _____

Let's find out more about those countries that use metrics in manufacturing products. Let's go on a metric scavenger hunt!

Directions: List ten products found in your home, such as a clock, chair, radio, watch, foods, and so on. Once the list is completed, search the item to find out where it was made. Write the origin next to each item you list.

	ITEM	*ORIGIN*
1.		
2.		
3.		
4.		
5.		
6.		
7.		
8.		
9.		
10.		

2-6 I WANT TO METER (4-6)

Objective: After completing this activity the student will be able to describe and use a metric ruler.

Materials Needed:

- 1 meterstick for each student

Procedure:

1. Explain the metric ruler. One meter consists of 100 centimeters or 10 decimeters. There are 10 millimeters in a centimeter.
2. Share the following information:

Unit Length	Value
Kilometer (km)	1,000 meters
Hectometer (hm)	100 meters
Dekameter (dam)	10 meters
Meter (m)	1 meter
Decimeter (dm)	1/10 or .1 meter or 10 centimeters
Centimeter (cm)	1/100 or .01 meter
Millimeter (mm)	1/1000 or .001 meter

2-7 DECIMETER JUMP (K-3)

Objective: After completing this activity the student should be able to describe and demonstrate the length of a decimeter.

Materials Needed:

- carpet squares
- permanent magic marker
- duct tape
- chart paper

Procedure:

1. Tape five or six carpet squares together with duct tape. Mark off and number decimeters with a permanent magic marker. Students can now jump in decimeters.
2. Graph the results.

2-8 METRIC MEASURING MANIA (4-6)

Objective: After completing this activity the student should be able to relate and use metric dimensions to detail an illustration.

Materials Needed:

- empty cereal boxes
- drawing paper
- crayons
- pencils
- metric ruler

Procedure:

1. Ask students to bring an empty cereal box to school. Using metric rulers, they should draw a copy of the empty cereal box. The drawing should be to scale.

2. Using a metric ruler, identify where the illustrations, titles, and ingredient listings are located. Include these details in your picture if possible, as shown in the illustration.

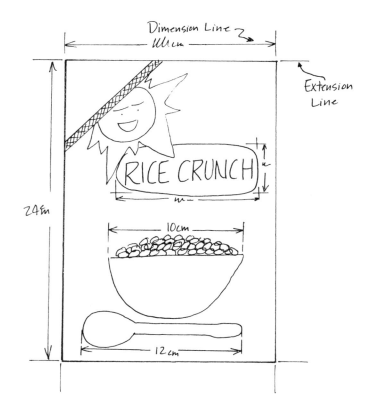

3. Explain dimension and extension lines and their use. They are often used in drafting. List dimensions to the side of the drawing. Extension lines extend out from ends of an object and serve as boundaries for dimension lines which show length, width, or depth.

4. Students will also want to use abbreviations for centimeter (cm) and possibly millimeter (mm).

5. Strive for perfection of detail. A sharp eye and keen metric rule can do wonders.

2-9 RESIDENTIAL DESIGN (4-6)

Objective: After completing this activity the student should be able to relate metric measurement to floor plan design.

Materials Needed:

- meter sticks
- meter walking wheels
- 18" × 25" drawing paper
- pencils

Procedure:

1. Discuss the concept of floor plan with students. All homes, apartments, and buildings have one. You may want to draw the floor plan of your own home or apartment as a demonstration. Explain that residential designers must identify the dimensions of rooms on a floor plan. These dimensions are used as a guide by builders. Include dimension lines, extension lines, and dimensions in the demonstration. Designs usually label rooms for ease of understanding.

2. After discussion, students can begin to develop a floor plan of their own home or apartment. Allow one to two weeks for completion. Floor plans should include:

> title
>
> student name
>
> floor plan drawing
>
> dimension lines in metric for at least two rooms
>
> labels for rooms
>
> appropriate symbols for doors
>
> work done in *pencil*

Consumer Math

This unit teaches math concepts while helping students become more intelligent and better-informed consumers.

2-10 FOOD FORUM (4-6)

Objective: After completing this activity the student should be able to design an evaluation instrument which includes unit price, quantity, and taste.

Materials Needed:

- paper
- pencils

Procedure:

1. Ask the class to imagine themselves as part of a special commission chosen to find "best values" in the grocery stores of their community. Since we are going to be in the business of comparing products and determining the best buy, we must come up with a system of evaluation.
2. After discussion, design the evaluation instrument which should include unit price, amount/quantity of food, and taste.

2-11 FRUIT SEARCH (4-6)

Objective: After completing this activity the student should be able to compute the cost per ounce of a food item.

Materials Needed:

- three cans of fruit (same kind, but different brands)
- paper cups
- balance scales
- paper
- pencils

Procedure:

1. Our evaluation tool has excited the community. They want to use it to compare three popular canned fruits. We must use the evaluation instrument to find the best product.

2. Find the unit price to determine the best buy in terms of cost per ounce. To do this, divide the number of ounces into the price of the item. Record the unit prices.

3. Next, open the cans and pour the liquid into three cups which have been marked with the name of each company. Determine which brand has the least syrup, most, etc. Discuss whether or not the customer would choose to buy the brand that contains more fruit or more sugared water.

4. Pass out samples of the fruit to make a taste test. Record opinions and rate the different brands.

5. Evaluate the three areas of assessment and vote for the best brand of fruit in terms of unit price, amount of fruit, and taste.

2-12 AD VANTAGE (4-6)

Objective: After completing this activity the student should be able to compute the sale price of an item.

Materials Needed:

- newspapers with ads
- scissors
- paste
- 18″ × 24″ paper
- pencils

Procedure:

1. Find ads that show "cents off." Have students cut out the ads and paste them to the large sheet of paper. Next to the ad, the children will determine the original price and decide if the sale item is a good buy. Encourage the students to find comparable items and compare sale prices. This activity can be expanded to include fractions and percentages.

2. The children can also discover a sale price by subtracting the amount off from the original price. For example, "30% off" will require finding 30% of the regular price, then subtracting that from the original to determine the sale price. This is a valuable tool in helping the students to become astute consumers.

3. A good follow-up to this activity may include pupil-designed ads which can be exchanged. Each student can give a set of problems to a friend to be worked on and returned for grading.

2-13 GOODS AND SERVICES (4-6)

Objective: After completing this activity the student should be able to describe the differences between goods and services.

Materials Needed:

- cloth
- yarn
- pins
- thread

- pencils
- needles
- paper

Procedure:

1. This activity helps students understand the difference between goods and services as well as the planning and organization required to make a business successful. Divide the class into two groups and form companies. The goods company will decide on a product that can be produced at home and marketed in the neighborhood. The other company will choose a service that each child can give on an individual basis in his/her neighborhood.

2. The goods company will need to create a simple product that can be produced with very inexpensive or no-cost materials. For example, cloth bags with yarn drawstrings for holding pens and pencils can be made easily by elementary school children. These materials are readily available in many households.

3. Since most school systems will not allow individual students to keep the profits, a contribution can be made to the school library in the name of the students in that company. When each group has made its final tally, divide the amount earned by the number of students in that company to determine what each student's profit would have been. Record and compare the results.

4. Follow up this experiment with a discussion of the time, money, and effort required to produce a product or provide a service. What adjustments were needed? What changes would help improve sales? What part did advertising play in the process? How did the goods or services help promote the quality of life?

2-14 LET'S EAT OUT! (4-6)

Objective: After completing this activity the student should be able to compute the cost of a meal ordered from a menu.

Materials Needed:

- menus from local restaurants
- teacher-made bills similar to those used in restaurants
- white paper plates
- crayons
- 18″ × 24″ white paper
- paste
- stapler

Procedure:

1. Each child will pick a menu and choose items to complete a meal. He/she will fill out the bill by writing in the food and drink ordered and the price per item. Add up the bill to find a subtotal (older children can determine the sales tax for a more accurate accounting). Record the tip and add all figures to find the grand total.

2. On the paper plate the student will draw and color the items ordered. Glue the plate to a large sheet of paper (this becomes the placemat). Finish by drawing the beverage, silverware and napkin. Staple the bill to the placemat and display in the classroom.

3. Another exciting idea is to use picture cut-outs from *Gourmet* or *Bon Apetit* or other magazines featuring meal planning, and arrange and glue the pictures to the paper plate for an appetizing look.

2-15 WHAT'S IN IT? (4-6)

Objective: After completing this activity the student should be able to comprehend product labels.

Materials Needed:

- empty boxes and cans with labels
- paper
- pencils
- teacher-made task cards

1. Prepare cards which ask the student to find answers to such questions as: "Which ingredient is in the greatest proportion?", "How many calories are there in a serving?", "How many preservatives or additives are there in this product?", "What company makes this item?", "Are there any warnings written on the label? If so, what are they?"

2. Accumulate approximately 25 containers and set out on a large table. Put task cards in an attractive display box. "Advertise" by hanging a large sign from the ceiling which will attract students to the table.

3. Follow this activity with a discussion of label awareness. Children will be amazed to discover what actually goes into a product.

Environmental Geometry

The origin of geometry is unknown; however, it is believed to have begun with the study of measurement. This unit's focus is the world of geometry. The activities, which encourage observation, comparison, and analysis, were developed to optimize experiential learning and provide a basic understanding of environmental geometry.

2-16 SHAPES ALIVE BRAINDRAWING (K-3)

Objective: After completing this activity the student should be able to identify closed and open shapes.

Materials Needed:

- chart paper
- pencil for each child

Procedure

1. Ask students to think of different geometric shapes (closed shapes) and line designs (open shapes). Their ideas must be drawn on a large shared sheet of paper.
2. The ground rules are as follows:

   There is to be no talking.

   Any idea must be drawn on the paper.

   Participants are encouraged to draw ideas which utilize other students' drawings.

   Quantity is desired.

   All ideas should be accepted non-verbally.

   No critical frowns.

   Original wild drawings are encouraged.

2-17 SHAPE SCIENTISTS (K-3)

Objective: After completing this activity the student should be able to organize geometric drawings into categories.

Materials Needed:

- copies of "Geometry in Nature Research Sheet"
- pencils

Procedure:

1. Ask each student to select four closed geometric shapes and four open shapes from the braindrawing list from the previous activity. These selections will serve as the raw material for students' geometric drawings. The eight shapes should be drawn in the spaces at the top of the "Geometry in Nature Research Sheet."

2. Now it is time to take a nature walk and write the names of objects in nature which have their eight shapes. The research sheet might look like the sample here when completed.

3. Share and discuss results. Were any categories difficult to find in nature? Why?

◯ (1)	△ (2)	▢ (3)	⬭ (4)	⌒ (5)	⌒ (6)	৪ (7)	⟋ (8)
tree trunk	leaf point	tree limb	bird's body	squirrel's tail	flower petal	animal's tail	flower petal
bird's beak	bird's beak	flower stem	bird's egg				
squirrel's eye			flower petal				
dandelion stem							

GEOMETRY IN NATURE RESEARCH SHEET

Name _____

Date _____

○ (1)	△ (2)	☐ (3)	⬭ (4)	S (5)	C (6)	⌀ (7)	⋀ (8)

2-18 OUTDOOR WONDERLAND (K-3)

Objective: After completing this activity, the student should be able to describe geometric shapes in the outdoors.

Materials Needed:

- camera
- film
- posterboard

- magic markers
- ruler

Procedure:

1. As you already may have discovered, there is no better source than the outdoors for discovering naturally created angles, shapes, and symmetrical forms. Once keyed to looking for geometric constructs, children will readily identify a multitude of natural sources of symmetry, angle, and shapes. This activity further builds on outdoor geometry.

2. Ask students to select a category from the "Sources of Geometry in Nature" list. Once selected, students should develop a photo essay of the shapes, angles, and symmetric/asymmetric forms of their chosen area. Students should strive to be creative with their presentation. Here are some examples:

Honeycombs and beehives	Trees—leaves—rings—branches
Sunflowers	Stalactites and stalagmites
Spider webs and spiders	Sand dunes and the slope of beaches
Pinecones	Ice crystals and snow
Sea shells and sea urchins	Ant hills
Sand dollars	Butterflies
Rocks and minerals	Fish scales and fins—movement
Star fish	Insects—legs—body
Fruits and vegetables	Light properties
Feathers	Erosion
Ferns	Cells

This is a starting point for identifying natural geometric principles.

2-19 SHAPE ARTISTRY (K-3)

Objective: After completing this activity the student should be able to design a picture that incorporates geometric shapes.

Materials Needed:

- 8½" × 11" drawing paper
- crayons

Procedure:

1. The students have had an opportunity to look closely at nature and see how their chosen geometric shapes fit in. Explain that they are now going to draw a picture of an animal, plant, or mineral.

2. There is one restriction, however. The picture can only use the geometric shapes included on the research sheet previously completed. Any combination of shapes is permitted. For example, a student might choose to make a bird. Using the shapes shown in the sample research sheet, the drawing might look like the illustration shown here. Note that the size of the shapes can be varied.

3. Discuss, compare, and contrast the students' drawings.

2-20 GEOMETRIC RECURSION (K-3)

Objective: After completing this activity, the student should be able to demonstrate with manipulatives the concept of recursion.

Materials Needed:

- toy set of wooden dowels, joints, wheels, etc.
- white glue
- examples of geometric recursion

Procedure:

1. Describe recursion by way of analogies—a picture that includes a picture of itself is an example of recursion. Students might also appreciate the recursion riddle: If you have two wishes, what is the second? (Two more wishes.) Discuss.

2. Begin by collecting data. Using journals, illustrations, photographs, and found objects, identify examples of geometric recursion (the repetition of a geometric form). Some examples are obvious, such as the honeycomb; others are more subtle. What is the geometric recursion of baby's breath (the flower)? Are there geometric recursions in sound, smell, taste, or movement?

3. Have students model a geometric recursion through the use of clay or toy manipulatives (Legos). Ask students to share their results.

2-21 SHAPES RECIPES (K-3)

Objective: After completing this activity, the student should be able to develop plans for a shapes recipe card.

Materials Needed:

- one 4″ × 6″ index card for each student
- pencils

Procedure:

Here's how to cook up some shapes recipes. Explain how each student is to design a recipe card. Students should compose a recipe that lists the shapes and varieties to be used in their nature drawing. The recipe sentence should utilize the following pattern: What animal, plant, or mineral can you create by combining one circle, one oval, seven triangles, three (another shape), one (another shape), and four rectangles?

2-22 SHARING RECIPES (K-3)

Objective: After completing this activity the student should be able to utilize written directions to compose a drawing.

Materials Needed:

- completed recipe cards
- 8½″ × 11″ drawing paper

- pencils
- crayons

Procedure:

1. Turn the completed recipe cards face down. Mix. Each student should pick a recipe card and attempt a drawing which uses all the ingredients. Good luck!
2. Discuss the drawings once they are completed. How difficult or easy was this activity?

2-23 REPEATING PATTERNS COLLAGE (K-3)

Objective: After completing this activity the student should be able to describe a repeating pattern.

Materials Needed:

- architecture and nature magazines
- 11½″ × 18″ drawing paper

- scissors

- glue

Procedure:

1. Ask students to search for repeating patterns in plant, animal, or mineral pictures in the magazines which have been provided. Create a collage of repeating patterns using photographs from magazines.
2. Share and discuss.

2-24 SHAPES MOVEMENTS (K-3)

Objective: After completing this activity the student should be able to relate patterns to movement.

Materials Needed:

- markers
- large sheets of drawing paper

- music

Procedure:

1. Have each student move across the floor to the accompaniment of music. After everyone has had a chance to move, ask the children to draw their movements on the paper provided. They can use any combination of colors.

2. Share and discuss the results. What movements and patterns do animals and plants make as they move?

2-25 FRACTALS (K-3)

Objective: After completing this activity the student should be able to relate pattern to the concept of fractals.

Materials Needed:

- December 1983 issue of *Smithsonian*
- paper
- pencils

Procedure:

1. Read and discuss the Jeanne McDermit article in the December 1983 issue of *Smithsonian,* "Geometrical Forms Known as Fractals, Finding Sense in Chaos." After the discussion, brainstorm, on the chalkboard, a list of possible chaotic forms which might qualify as fractals.
2. Ask students to pair up and select an item from the list, and cooperatively work to identify some geometric pattern of recursion in the object. It may be helpful to students to pick an item from the list which could be observed firsthand. This will facilitate their analysis.
3. Have each team share their results.

2-26 PLAYGROUND GEOMETRY I (K-3)

Objective: After completing this activity the student should be able to relate previously learned geometric concepts to playground design.

Materials Needed: to be negotiated

Procedure:

1. Once a student understands the concepts, he or she is ready to manipulate and create. Spend a short time brainstorming a list of different types of playground structures. Discuss which ones are the favorites.
2. Ask students to design new playground equipment utilizing all their new information. The designs can incorporate geometric recursion (repetition), geometric patterns, fractals, and/or utilize nature's designs. Encourage the designers to be creative and wildly original. Their designs do not need to make sense. Students should have no boundaries for their designs and can choose to portray their ideas through any media.

3. The teacher may choose to introduce at a later time constraints on the design process such as money, construction time available, materials, and/ or feasibility of idea. Students would then need to evaluate their designs based on these criteria.

2-27 PLAYGROUND GEOMETRY II (K-3)

Objective: After completing this activity the student should be able to relate geometric concepts to a model design.

Materials Needed:

- tires of various sizes
- bolts from 2″ to 18″ in length
- brace and ¼″ bit
- washers (must fit bolts)
- nuts (must fit bolts)

Procedure:

This activity requires that the students incorporate geometric recursion in their design. They are also limited in terms of potential building materials. Only tires, bolts (2″–6″), and washers can be used. You may choose to have students form teams to develop a design. Use the brace and bit to form holes in tires for the bolts. While this activity would require some advance planning (obtaining materials) it is a creative and exciting way to put into practice what the students have learned about geometry.

Numeralonics

Numbers are everywhere. We rarely stop to think about where they came from or how they could be changed. This unit will cause the student to stop, think, and create.

2-28 MAKE A LOGO (K-3)

Objective: After completing this activity, the student should be able to define a cardinal number.

Materials Needed:

- 8½″ × 11″ white paper
- crayons and markers
- paintbrushes
- tempera paints
- construction paper
- glue
- scissors

Procedure:

1. Begin by explaining that the number of elements in a set is often called the *cardinal number* of a set. A set of five juicy apples would be associated with the cardinal number 5. Any set in one-to-one correspondence with the set of juicy apples would have a cardinal number 5 associated with it.

2. Imagine that a company which manufactures toys is interested in a new logo for their firm. They produce ten different kinds of toys: balls, bats, trains, dolls, tracks, building sets, stuffed animals, puppets, cars, and blocks. Members of the class have been asked to design a new logo. The company has asked that the logo incorporate *at least* two toys they design and a cardinal number beside the toys. Ask each student to design their logo on an

8½″ × 11″ sheet. The logo should use most of the space on the sheet. Any coloring technique is acceptable: crayons, watercolors, construction paper, tempera, felt tips. Each student's name and age should be included on the back of the logo. Good luck!

2-29 LOGO RODEO (K-3)

Objective: After completing this activity the student should be able to substantiate why their logo warrants an award.

Materials Needed:

- completed logos
- teacher-made awards

Procedure:

1. Everyone has created a logo. What creativity! Now it is time to share. Each student should demonstrate why their logo is well suited to the company's needs. Attention can be given to the logo's originality, color complementarity, and its ability to catch the eye from a distance. As each student shares, ask the audience to participate by sharing what they perceive as strengths of the logo.

2. Distribute awards to everyone. Suggested award titles are: Original, Color-wise, and Catch That Eye. Give several awards for each category. Everyone is a winner.

2-30 THE NATURE OF NUMBER/NUMERAL (K-3)

Objective: After completing this activity the student should be able to develop a large list of alternative numeral names.

Materials Needed:

- 8½″ × 11″ paper
- pencils

Procedure:

1. Giving word names to numbers is part of an evolutionary process that is still going on today. The following activity removes several restrictions on the student's thinking about numbers and will yield some interesting results.

2. A numeral is the *written symbol* or *spoken name* to express the concept of number. Explain that the numbers used by ancient and modern civilizations are the same, only the names (numerals) have changed. Also, numbers have many acceptable names (e.g., 4, 12/3). In pairs, students should pick a

numeral between 1 and 20. Each pair should compile a list of alternative names for their numeral. Remind students of the definition of numeral—the written symbol or spoken name to express the concept of number.

3. Encourage students to form a lengthy list, the more the better. Seek the unusual! Share and discuss each pair's results.

2-31 NUMERAL TIME MACHINE (K-3)

Objective: After completing this activity the student should be able to imagine and interpret how numerals were used in history.

Materials Needed:

- overhead projector
- transparency

Procedure:

1. We are going to take a look at the development of numerals. Our time machine will allow us to quickly discover the numerals used by great cultures. Take the students on a guided fantasy back in time. How does life change? How are numerals important? Imagine walking through an ancient marketplace. Why are numerals important? After ample time has been taken to travel in the time machine, ask the students to return to the classroom.

2. Discuss and record the many ways the students imagined numerals being used. If you lack experience with "guided fantasy" as an instructional technique, you could use a written excerpt from literature which describes a specific period in time.

English	Egyptian	Greek	Babylonian	Roman	Hindu/Arabic
					0
Zero					1
One	I	A	▼	I	2
	II	B	▼▼	II	3
	III	Γ	▼▼▼	III	4
	IIII	Δ	▼▼▼▼	IV	5
Five	III II	E	▼▼▼ ▼▼	V	6
	III III	F	▼▼▼ ▼▼▼	VI	7
	IIII III	Z	▼▼▼ ▼▼▼▼	VII	8
	IIII IIII	H	▼▼▼ ▼▼▼	VIII	9
Nine	III III III	Θ	▼▼▼ ▼▼▼	IX	10
Ten	⋂	I	◁	X	
One Hundred	𐤒	P	▼▷	C	100

3. How are the numeral systems similar? How are they different? Can you guess which numeration system is the oldest? How about the most recent?

2-32 I GOT THE SYSTEM (K-3)

Objective: After completing this activity the students should be able to develop their own numeration system.

Materials Needed:

- dependent on creativity of students...be prepared

Procedure:

1. Now it's our turn to create a numeration system. The system should include 0–10 and 100. Encourage students to stretch their imagination. No idea is too wild. The system can take any form. This leaves a wide open field for creativity. Mention to students that the original definition of numeral—any written symbol or spoken name—is temporarily being suspended in order to encourage creativity.

2. Provide time to share, compare, and discuss the numeration systems once they are completed. Further activities might involve use of the created numeration system to do addition, subtraction, multiplication, and division. The possibilities are endless.

Math
Happenings

Community resources provide many opportunities for students to gain an understanding of practical applications of mathematics in businesses, professions, and services. This unit includes activities presented during a week dedicated to the practical applications of math. Members of the business community come into the classroom to share how they use math in their work. Students engage in different math-related activities each day of the week to develop skills, enrichment, and competition. This unit may be used with several classes for a week or with one class for a longer period of time. Throughout the unit, students will apply math skills in completing activities, listening to guest speakers, competing in a math contest, and writing thank-you letters.

The "Math Week" activities can be easily planned by using these suggestions:

1. Decide on the date for math week, allowing ample time for securing speakers.

2. Plan appropriate activities for the involved students.

3. Collect materials and prepare activities.

4. Make a schedule so that each class devotes one period per day to the planned activity for the day.

5. Invite a speaker for each class for the same period on a chosen day. Be sure to get confirmation from speakers.

6. If students are to teach a class, begin working with them to prepare a lesson plan and practice.

7. Explain "Math Happenings Week" to involved teachers.

8. Announce the week's activities to students through teachers and posters of the daily happenings.

9. Prepare competition activities, reserve a large place (media center or gym) where competition will be held, and engage a person to assist at each station.

Gather these materials for "Math Week":

- rulers
- yardsticks
- metersticks
- measurement tapes
- liquid containers
- popcorn
- candy
- rope
- several sets of earphones

- tape players
- helium-filled balloons
- notes for balloons
- tangrams
- transparencies
- overhead projectors
- graph paper
- helium

2-33 MEASUREMENT MONDAY (K-3)

Objective: After completing this activity the student should be able to use various measurement devices.

Materials Needed:

- rulers
- tape measures
- paper

- yardsticks
- metersticks
- pencils

Procedure:

Using rulers, tapes, yardsticks, and metersticks, students should measure designated areas to find heights, lengths, areas, and volumes which they record.

2-34 STUDENT TEACHING TUESDAY (K-3)

Objective: After completing this activity the student should be able to teach a chosen math lesson.

Materials Needed:

- paper
- pencils

- sample lessons

Procedure:

Students who enjoy math can work in pairs to prepare a unique lesson and teach it to a class. The lesson should include a title, learning outcome, list of needed materials, a description of the activity, and a means of evaluation— "how successful was the lesson?"

2-35 WORKERS' WEDNESDAY (K-3)

Objective: After completing this activity the student should be able to describe how math is used in the business world.

Materials Needed:

- resource persons

Procedure:

Each classroom will have a different speaker who will share how he/she uses math in his/her work. Speakers should be chosen from a variety of jobs to share how math affects their work.

During the following week have students write thank-you letters to guest speakers using proper letter form.

2-36 TRY TO GUESS THURSDAY (K-3)

Objective: After completing this activity the student will be able to make estimates.

Materials Needed:

- popcorn
- rope
- paper
- plastic bag
- scale
- pencils

Procedure:

Set up several estimating activities where students submit their estimates secretly so a winner can be determined. Estimates could be made for pieces of candy or popcorn in a container or plastic bag, the number of cups of water in a large container, the length of a coiled rope or wire, the area of a wall, the height of a structure, or the weight of an object.

2-37 FAR AWAY FRIDAY (K-3)

Objective: After completing this activity the student should be able to pinpoint various locations on a map.

Materials Needed:

- pencil
- paper
- helium-filled heavy-duty balloons
- state map
- stamped, addressed post cards

Procedure:

This activity is planned to determine which balloon travels the greatest distance when notes are returned. Each student will write his/her name and address on a stamped post card asking that finder write name and location and drop in a mailbox. The notes will be placed in balloons. Allowing all students to release their balloons at the same time makes an exciting experience. Release the balloons after the "Math-Go-Round." The notes may be placed on a large map of the state as they are returned.

2-38 MATH-GO-ROUND (K-3)

Objective: After completing this activity the student should be able to record answers to various problems.

Materials Needed:

- tangrams
- tape recorders
- taped math problems

- prepared answer sheets
- rulers
- large arena area

Procedure:

On Friday or the last day of activities, set up stations in a large area where small groups of students move from one station to another to solve word problems; listen to taped addition, subtraction, multiplication, and division problems which must be solved in a timed test; weigh and measure items; and put together tangrams. Students record answers on prepared sheets for each station and a winner is determined by a student's overall score for each class. One class at a time participates in the competition activities.

2-39 CALCULATOR CHATTER AND BABBLES (4-6)

Objective: After completing this activity the student should be able to solve math problems to the design of a "Babble."

Materials Needed:

- hand-held calculators

Procedure:

1. "Babbles" is a great logic activity. Students will apply mathematical concepts as they invent their own "Babbles" (stories) using the calculator.

Have the class first compile a list of words that can be displayed on a calculator when the numbers are viewed *upside down.* Reproduce individual or group Babbles in booklet form. Students will have fun reading stories and solving math problems with the calculator.

0 = 0	5 = S
1 = i	6 = g
2 = Z	7 = L
3 = E	8 = B
4 = h	

2. Try this "Babble" by two 4th graders...

The eating contest will take place on a $1000 \div 8 \times 3 + 400 + 3 - 160 =$ _____ $70 \times 100 + 700 - 333 + 444 - 11 - 86 =$ _____ in Cleveland, .0140. The judge walked on the stage and said, "The contestants are: $900 - 92 =$ _____, $8000 - 282 =$ _____, $32000 - 427 =$ _____, $46000 + 137 =$ _____, $317500 + 37 =$ _____, and $400 - 63 =$ _____."

The object of the contest is to eat the $9000 - 4000 + 663 =$ _____ that the moms will $9000 - 1500 - 92 - 300 =$ _____. The kids can't eat the $80000 - 3000 + 345 =$ _____, so they will have to peel them.

Then the contest began. The contestants made $10000 - 4000 - 500 + 104 =$ _____ of themselves. They started to $400000 - 30000 + 8806 =$ _____ down the $10000 - 5000 + 663 =$ _____.

After the race was over, the judge said, "$65536 - 255 =$ _____ want a word with the winner, $900 - 92 =$ _____." After the judge waited about five minutes, he decided that $800 - 766 =$ _____ wasn't going to speak to him.

Architecture Around Us

2-40 WHAT'S HAPPENING HERE (K-3)

Objective: After completing this activity the student should be able to demonstrate compression.

Materials Needed:

- sponges
- chart paper

- magic marker

Procedure:

1. Compression is an ever-present force at work in our daily lives. When materials are pressed together, compression is at work. If you are observant, you will recognize compression everywhere.

2. Demonstrate how a wet sponge loses water when compression is applied. Ask students to form pairs. Each pair must create a way of demonstrating compression at work through the use of body-centered geometry. (See the illustrations for examples.) Ideas will be generated quickly. Students should share their representations.

3. Great! Everyone has had an opportunity to share an example of body-centered compression. Were there any other examples of compression at work while students were sharing (e.g., back compressed to floor). Finish the lesson by brainstorming examples of compression at work in the classroom. Examples might include the wall, a chair, yourself, books, shelves, and the legs of desks. Write the ideas on a large sheet of chart paper.

2-41 PULLING APART AN IDEA (K-3)

Objective: After completing this activity the student should be able to demonstrate tension.

Materials Needed:

- string
- rubber band
- chart paper
- magic markers

Procedure:

1. In architecture, tension is a stress on a material produced by a pull of forces tending to cause extension. Tension is at work everywhere.

2. Demonstrate how tension occurs when a string and rubber band are pulled. Ask the students to again form pairs. They must again use body-centered geometry to demonstrate tension, as shown in the illustration. Students should share their representations.

3. Brainstorm all the possible examples of tension in the classroom. Compare and contrast the compression list with the tension list. Examples might include a clothesline holding up student work, paper, the middle of a shelf, or a wall hanging.

2-42 CHAIRPERSON (K-3)

Objective: After completing this activity the student should be able to identify points on a chair where compression and tension exist.

Materials Needed:

- scissors
- glue
- magazines
- construction paper

Procedure:

Many chairs beautifully demonstrate tension and compression at work. The following activity will help students collect and organize data:

1. Have students begin by choosing a photograph of a chair from a magazine. Cut out the photograph and glue to a construction paper backing.
2. Make up a list of questions which might be asked about the chair (e.g., where is the compression greatest? Are there any examples of tension?).
3. Have the students pretend they are the chair. Where is there compression and tension?
4. Mark areas of the chair where compression and tension are noted. (See the illustration.)

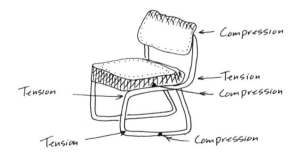

5. Ask students if they can make a hypothesis based on where they predicted compression and tension would occur. Sample hypotheses might include:

- Compression exists where objects are joined.
- Bends in materials may have tension.
- Bends in materials may have compression.
- Compression is everywhere.
- We can cause compression and tension.

2-43 BY WAY OF THE BRIDGE (K-3)

Objective: After completing this activity the students should be able to design their own bridge.

Materials Needed:

- one box (2000-count) tongue depressors, pre-drilled on each end with a ⅛″ bit (*Tip:* drill four to five depressors at a time)
- brads
- balsa blocks

- photographs of bridges
- construction paper
- glue
- markers
- 2″ × 2″ × 2″ cardboard

Procedure:

Ask students to study independently the attributes of bridges. They should pay particular attention to examples of tension and compression. During their research and synthesis they should do the following:

1. Examine photographs or illustrations of bridges.
2. Mount photos and make written predictions of where tension and compression might exist.
3. Identify a minimum of five attributes of the bridge. Examples of attributes might include length, material, trusses, arches, piers, color, shape, size, and function.
4. Design a bridge which is unique in some way using tongue depressors, balsa blocks, cardboard (2″ × 2″ × 2″) and brads. An example is shown in the illustration. During the design process the student might focus on ways to modify, magnify, minimize, substitute, rearrange, combine, or reverse.

2-44 LOAD IT ON...1 (K-3)

Objective: After completing this activity the student should be able to build human sculptures to demonstrate load.

Materials Needed:

- 8½″ × 11″ mimeograph paper
- two dictionaries
- 10-gram weights (or use pennies)
- chart paper
- markers

Procedure:

1. In architecture, load is the weight that a structure can hold. This concept can be demonstrated beautifully with one sheet of construction paper. Place the paper between two dictionaries. The distance between the books should be 5″ to 8″. Add a 10-gram weight. The paper will fall. The load was too great. Loads are everywhere. Part of the job of an architect is knowing how much load a building can accommodate.

2. Ask the children to form triads and invent ways to demonstrate load by making a human sculpture. (See the illustration.) This is a lot of fun and gets the point across. Imagine the possible formations. Have the triads share their discoveries.

3. Now it is time to brainstorm examples of load. Write the ideas on a large sheet of chart paper.

2-45 LOAD IT ON...2 (K-3)

Objective: After completing this activity the student should be able to build and test a beam.

Materials Needed:

- white glue
- 8½" × 11" construction paper
- scissors
- dictionaries
- 10-gram weights (or use pennies)

Procedure:

1. Review the previous experiment. The paper sheet fell when a minimum of weight was added. Our goal for today is to examine ways to reinforce the paper so that greater loads can be carried. The I-beam is a popular construction material which utilizes the I-design as a means of increasing its strength. This design can be recreated by cutting the 8½" × 11" paper in half. Fold each half into thirds and glue the halves together on the middle third. It should look like this:

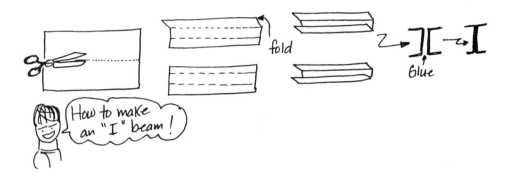

2. Ask the students to make predictions as to how many grams the I-beam will hold. Place the paper I-beam on two dictionaries. There should be a 6" distance between the dictionaries. Add weights until the load is so great that the I-beam structure collapses. How close were the predictions? Examine the I-beam structure. Where did the structure bend?

2-46 LOAD IT ON...3 (K-3)

Objective: After completing this activity the student should be able to build and test his or her own paper beam.

Materials Needed:

- white glue
- 8½" × 11" construction paper
- dictionaries
- pencils
- 10-gram weights (or use pennies)
- scissors
- rulers
- copies of "Gram Graph" sheets

Procedure:

1. Review the previous lesson. The I-beam certainly has its merits. Now it is the students' turn. Give each student one sheet of construction paper, glue, and scissors along with the following directions:

- Design a beam that can support a load.
- The sheet of paper can be cut and glued in any fashion.
- The final product must be able to span the 6-inch distance between the two dictionaries.

2. Once all designs are completed, distribute the "Gram Graph" sheets.

3. Have each student draw individual designs under the appropriate name, as shown in the illustration.

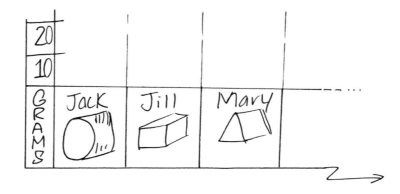

4. It is now time for each student to test his or her design. Students observing the results should fill in the graph for each student once a structure collapses. (See illustration.)

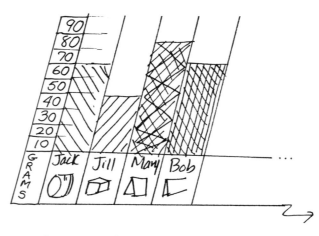

5. Compare and contrast the results. What conclusions can be drawn?

GRAM GRAPH

GRAMS						
240						
230						
220						
210						
200						
190						
180						
170						
160						
150						
140						
130						
120						
110						
100						
90						
80						
70						
60						
50						
40						
30						
20						
10						

RESEARCH TOPICS FOR FURTHER STUDY OF "MATH AMAZING"

Presented here are a collection of provocative topics requiring a curious mind. The topics are designed to encourage divergent as well as convergent thinking. *Beware:* young researchers may end up detouring into uncharted waters of knowledge and inquiry. The teacher/facilitator should encourage and welcome these departures.

1. Compare and contrast natural bridges and architecturally designed bridges. (This can be done with any natural form and any person-created design.)

2. Design a roller coaster based on research of stress and structure design. Create a scale model of your roller coaster track.

3. Study the structural design of water and fire towers. Compare the structures and purposes of each. Investigate nature's balancing rocks. Compare this natural wonder to the towers studied. Create a model water tower.

4. Research pyramids and their construction. Pyramids are said to have mystical powers. Construct a small pyramid greenhouse and a geodesic dome greenhouse. These can be small and work as hot houses do. Conduct a study comparing the effects on plants with each structural style.

5. Using Thale's method of figuring the height of the great pyramid, compute the height of objects near your school.

6. Bicycle wheels are effective by using spokes for stress and tension. Explain how they support weight and how they are constructed. Develop a wheel for a bicycle that will support a large amount of weight for a cross-country tour.

7. Airplane pilots use geometry in many ways. Discover the many uses of geometry in the aerospace industry.

BIBLIOGRAPHY FOR "MATH AMAZING"

Architecture Without Architects by Barnard Rudofsky (New York: Museum of Modern Art; Doubleday, 1964).

The Calculating Book by James T. Rogers (New York: Random House, 1975).

Calculators Computers—A Sourcebook of Activities by Don Inman (Reading, MA: Addison-Wesley, 1976).

City: Pyramids: Cathedral by David Macaulay (Boston: Houghton Mifflin, 1974).

Fantastic Calculator Math by Edward C. Beardslee (San Jose, CA: Enrich, 1978).

"Geometrical Forms Known as Fractals Find Sense in Chaos" by Jeanne McDermitt *(Smithsonian,* Volume 14, No. 9, December 1983, 110).

Geometry for Teachers by Ward Bouwsa (New York: Macmillan, 1972).

Kid's America by Steven Caney (New York: Workman Publishing, 1978).

"Penny Power" *(Penny Power Magazine,* 256 Washington Street, Mount Vernon, NY 10550, August/September 1982).

Section 3

WRITING WISELY

Sound writing skills are essential. The activities in this chapter will provide a firm foundation for students to build upon as they learn how to "construct" effective and creative compositions. From imaginative approaches to poetry writing to activities which teach the steps of the writing process—prewriting, writing, editing, revising, rewriting, and proofreading—your students will acquire many new writing skills. Just imagine writing a court case related to the parts of speech...

ACTIVITY TITLE AND GRADE LEVEL	SKILLS USED
The Writing Process	
3-1 Prewriting (4-6)	collecting and organizing data
3-2 Writing (4-6)	classifying; summarizing
3-3 Editing/Revising (4-6)	classifying; criticizing
3-4 Evaluation (4-6)	interpreting; comparing; criticizing
Brew, Balloons, and Doodles	
3-5 Witch's Brew (4-6)	imagining; collecting and organizing data; classifying
3-6 Balloons, Balloons, Balloons! (4-6)	collecting and organizing data; comparing; classifying
3-7 Describe a Doodle (4-6)	collecting and organizing data; comparing; criticizing

ACTIVITY TITLE AND GRADE LEVEL	SKILLS USED
Creative Writing: A+	
3-8 September—Success in the UFL (4-6)	classifying; collecting and organizing data; imagining
3-9 October—Thoughts in the Cave (4-6)	imagining; hypothesizing; looking for assumptions
3-10 November—Story Starters (4-6)	imagining; looking for assumptions; hypothesizing
3-11 December—What's in a Card? (4-6)	imagining; looking for assumptions; hypothesizing
3-12 Spring in January (4-6)	imagining; classifying
3-13 February—Valid Valentines (4-6)	imagining; criticizing
3-14 March—Soaring Ideas (4-6)	Imagining; collecting and organizing data; comparing; criticizing
3-15 April—Crack Me Open (4-6)	classifying; comparing; hypothesizing
3-16 May—Blooming Ideas (4-6)	imagining; collecting and organizing data
3-17 June—Creative Writing Plug-Ins (4-6)	imagining; collecting and organizing data
3-18 Parts of Speech File Fun (4-6)	collecting and organizing data; imagining; classifying

Topics for Further Study

Bibliography

The Writing Process: A Primer for Teachers

Writing may be thought of as the thread of commonality which spans the curriculum and ties up the subject area packages. Learning to write accurately and effectively is not only a valuable tool, it can be a pleasant experience as well. Students need opportunities to express their ideas daily and freely in a non-threatening environment where their ideas are accepted, where the writing process is used to develop their work, and where their work is published on walls, in halls, on bulletin boards, in booklets, or in books.

The writing process involves the following stages: prewriting, writing, editing, revising, rewriting, and proofreading to produce a finished composition. With patience and positive instruction students can learn to write *what they think and feel.*

3-1 PREWRITING (4-6)

Objective: After this activity the student should be able to generate ideas on a given writing topic.

Procedure:

1. Prewriting is a crucial stage in developing writing skills since it is during this time that students' imaginations are activated, ideas are expressed, interest and excitement are created, and everyone gleans ideas with which to begin writing. There are many strategies which can be used during this initial motivation stage, such as the following:

   thinking   role-playing

   observing   creating word banks

   discussing   brainstorming

   listing   viewing a film

imagining	drawing
listening	interviewing
remembering	working in pairs
researching	working in small groups

2. After students have ideas, words, and phrases about a topic, they are ready to begin the writing stage.

3-2 WRITING (4-6)

Objective: After this activity the student should be able to write a draft on a given topic.

Materials Needed:

- paper
- pencils

Procedure:

1. During the writing of the first draft, students simply pour out ideas without regard for spelling and mechanics at this time. An error-free paper is not the goal of this draft.
2. Not all writing assignments are to become finished compositions and those which are not should be placed in the student's individual writing folder possibly to be finished later, if so desired.
3. If a particular draft is to become a finished composition, the remaining stages of the writing process are to be continued.

3-3 EDITING/REVISING (4-6)

Objective: After this activity the student should be able to use an editing checklist to revise a first-draft manuscript.

Materials Needed:

- first drafts
- editing checklist
- pencils

Procedure:

1. After completing the first draft, students begin editing and revising their work. During this stage they work on their own and may add, delete, change,

rearrange, move sentences and paragraphs, check mechanics and spelling, and do anything else to correct and polish their writing. Then they may continue editing with a peer, in a small reading/writing group, or with the teacher.

2. An editing checklist made up by the teacher or by the teacher and students is helpful. Such a list might include the following items:

- Have I stuck to the topic? (unity)
- Does it make sense? (coherence)
- Did I use different sentence types and lengths?
- Check spelling.
- Check mechanics—capital letters and punctuation.
- Does the writing say something interesting?
- Have I said what I intended to say?

3. When students feel they have made their writing the best they can, have them write a *final copy*, proofread it, and rewrite it if necessary before publishing it.

Since students write best about topics with which they are familiar, it is wise to start the teaching of writing with such topics. They will have a lot to say about familiar topics and they can write well when properly motivated and instructed.

4. Interesting writing involves the use of "writers' tools" such as the following:

Simile—a comparison of two things or actions usually joined by "like," "as," or "than." Example: "cold as ice."

Metaphor—a name given to a person or thing that it is not. Example: "a jewel in the sky."

Personification—human characteristics given to inanimate objects. Example: "the wind howled."

Onomatopoeia—words that sound like their meanings. Examples: "buzz," "bop," "zing."

Synonyms—words with similar meanings, used to convey a more specific meaning. Example: "big; enormous."

Antonyms—words with opposite meanings. Example: "transparent; opaque."

Alliteration—repetition of sounds or words. Example: "bees buzzed busily."

Hyperbole—an exaggeration for effect. Example: "turned green with envy."

Irony—a humorous or sarcastic expression in which the literal meaning is the opposite of the intended meaning. Examples: "how beautiful" (actually ugly), "how clever" (actually stupid).

When students use these tools to help express ideas, their writings become alive, specific, and interesting.

3-4 EVALUATION (4-6)

Objective: After this activity the student should be able to identify positive comments and suggestions in an evaluation of his/her work.

Procedure:

1. Since writing is such a personal matter, it requires positive and informative comments and suggestions.
2. This is best accomplished by the use of positive editorial comments and questions by both the teacher and students. Many students become reluctant writers if everything is marked wrong on their papers. When content is considered valuable and the writing process is followed, students develop self-confidence about being successful writers.

Brew, Balloons, and Doodles

The following writing activities incorporate the writing process in original and effective ways.

3-5 WITCH'S BREW (4-6)

Objective: After completing this activity the student should be able to list/write directions for others to follow.

Materials Needed:

- a simple recipe on chart paper
- paper
- recipes students bring in
- pencils

Procedure:

Your students will really be "bewitched" with this activity! Using a recipe format, students can create their own recipe for a magic spell, a love potion, or any other special brew by listing and writing directions.

1. Display a recipe on chart paper and discuss the language of the recipe, noting the measurement abbreviations and words used in directions for putting the ingredients together. Call attention also to the form used in writing a recipe.

2. If this actually is done before Halloween, ask students to list some ingredients which might be appropriate for use by a witch in preparing a brew to be used in casting spells. (This lesson is also effective in February for creating recipes for love potions.) Write some suggested ingredients and direction words on the board.

3. Ask students to make a list of ingredients and the amounts they wish to use in their recipes.

4. Using their lists of selected ingredients, students write directions for combining the ingredients as well as whether to freeze, boil, bake, hide for a few days, drink, rub it on, or eat it.

5. Follow-Up Ideas: This writing may be illustrated and used in a display with a witch, a big cauldron, black cat, etc. Another idea for publishing is to compile the writings in a "Witch's Brew" booklet.

Stews, elixirs, or brews may be written for the following reasons:

> To Catch a Leprechaun
>
> To Make a Teacher Give All As
>
> To Be a Happy Person
>
> To Stop Wars

3-6 BALLOONS, BALLOONS, BALLOONS!!! (4-6)

Objective: After this activity the student should be able to use correct language and writing skills in a creative writing experience.

Materials Needed:

- balloons
- paper
- pencils

- Word Bank sheet
- string

Procedure:

In this creative writing activity students will combine previously learned language and writing skills to create a story about a "living balloon."

1. *Non-Stop Talking: A Prewriting Activity:*
   A. Display some blown-up balloons which have strings attached for easy handling. Arrange students in reading/writing (R/W) groups of four or five students in each group.

   Students then "Chatter Chatter Chatter" after receiving a balloon in each group. At the signal to begin, Person A in each group holds the balloon and begins to talk non-stop to the others in his group about the balloon he is holding. After 30 seconds, a signal indicates that Person B holds the balloon and talks non-stop. Then Person C and Person D have their turns. Each person should listen carefully to what is being said and try to say different things. Remember, don't stop talking until the signal is given.

   B. On the Word Bank sheet provided for each student, they write words heard during the "Chatter Chatter Chatter" period as well as words of their own, placing the words on the correct balloon. Students may check each other's balloons to determine if words have been correctly labeled if so desired. Each group may offer its favorite word or words from each category and these may be written on the board or on a transparency by the teacher for everyone to use.

   C. Ask students to close their eyes and use their imaginations as you lead them through some suggestions for creating a story about a balloon adventure. Walk them through some details for the story with questions such as the following:

- Pretend you have become a living balloon. How do you look? How do you feel?

- Suddenly, you start to move. How do you move? Where do you go? How does it feel? What do you see? What do you hear?

- You are a risk-taking balloon, so you have an adventure. What happens to you? Are you alone? Who else is there? Did you get into trouble? How did you solve your problem?

- Return to where you started. How did you get back? What was the trip like? Was someone there when you returned? Who was it?

- What happened when you returned? Did you become famous? Did you get into more trouble?

2. *Writing:* Students are now asked to write about an adventure as a "Living Balloon."

3. *Editing:* Have students edit their own papers before using peer or group editing.

4. *Revision:* Students may make any changes necessary to improve their writing. Then, they rewrite the work including corrections and changes and again edit their work.

5. *Final Copy or Finished Composition:* This is the copy written in ink that is the best they can make it.

6. *Proofread:* Proofread and if necessary rewrite.

7. *Publish:* Students value their work when they feel they have done their best and when it is displayed for others to enjoy.

3-7 DESCRIBE A DOODLE (4-6)

Objective: After this activity the student will be able to use descriptive words in writing directions.

Materials Needed:

- an individual copy of a "doodle" (an abstract design) for each student or group in the class
- 5" × 7" index cards
- pencils
- paper

Procedure:

This activity is designed to sharpen the student's ability to observe and describe accurately as well as provide practical experiences in writing and following directions.

1. *Prewriting:* Have the class talk through directions for doing something familiar, such as, making a peanut butter sandwich, tying a shoelace, or going from the classroom to the media center with emphasis on sequence.

Distribute a different copy of a "doodle" to each student. Instruct students to write step-by-step directions for reproducing the design or "doodle." Ask students to put the "doodle" card number at the top of their direction page.

2. *Writing:* Each student writes directions for reproducing a "doodle." When students have completed the writing assignment, the teacher redistributes the written directions to other students and takes up the "doodles" from each student.

Instruct students to reproduce the design, following the directions exactly, on a clean sheet of paper. Upon completion, the reproduction is attached to the directions and returned to the original writer. The original design is given to the writer also, and a comparison of the original and the reproduction is made to determine the reason for any variations.

3. *Editing/Revising:* Continue the steps of the writing process if this assignment is to become a "Doodle Booklet" or if it is done just for fun for other students.

4. *Evaluation:* Each set of directions may be reviewed by the teacher to determine whether discrepancies are a result of the directions or a result of different interpretations of the directions.

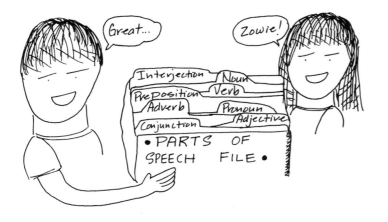

Creative Writing: A+

Creative writing is a combination of logical thought and original thought. This particular unit attempts to employ those thought processes. It is written for bulletin board or task card usage. Wherever possible, allow students to help with the design and ideas.

3-8 SEPTEMBER—SUCCESS IN THE UFL (4-6)

Objective: After this activity, the student should be able to use collected data to support proposed changes in the game of football.

Materials Needed:

- copies of football patterns with assignments written on them
- bulletin board
- paper
- pencils

Procedure:

Tell the class that they are members of the newly formed Universal Football League (UFL). As group members they will have several duties. Divide the group into three to five members and present them the same situations:

1. Research the history of football. List the highlights on a timeline.
2. Design a card game to teach the rules to someone who may not know how to play football.
3. Now that all members are familiar with the rules and history of football, present the following:

   a. You have volunteered to initiate several changes to improve the game of football. You may choose from the list on the bulletin board.

b. Changes: the color of the football, a nine-member team, different protective pads, a rule change.

c. You must support your reasons for your decisions. Convince others that your ideas would be to the benefit of the game.

It is not necessary for the groups to complete all of the changes. Allow writing with illustration.

4. *Evaluation:* Present the changes in a "Board Meeting" and have the students decide which of the changes would be the most beneficial for the game. Usually criteria can be set up ahead of time. For example, consider the reasons behind the changes explored. Are they valid reasons? Would they improve the game? Add more excitement?

3-9 OCTOBER—THOUGHTS IN THE CAVE (4-6)

Objective: After this activity, the student should be able to identify a certain characteristic of bats and write a short creative story on that characteristic.

Materials Needed:

- copies of bat pattern
- pencils
- bat cave made out of crumpled brown kraft paper
- thumbtacks
- string
- box to hold bats
- glue
- scissors

Procedure

1. Place the empty bat cave on the bulletin board. Put string and bats in a bat box on the table in front of the bulletin board. Students may choose which of the bats they would like to do. When they have written about the bat, tell them to attach the string and hang the bat in the cave, outside the cave, on the ceiling.

2. The following may be copied on the bats:

   — I was born without the ability to find my way between objects. What can I do?

   — I am afraid of the dark.

   — I was raised by the friendly bats.

   — I have a broken wing.

   — Most people are afraid of me so I don't have many friends. How can I have more friends?

   — I'm tired of eating insects. I will change my diet to...

   — Bats have no privacy.

   — Advantages of sleeping hanging upside down.

   — If I had a bat as a pet...

   — My knees bend backward while I'm on the ground. Can you imagine the problems I have?

3. You may like to just grade for a particular skill. (For example, underline four adjectives, or have one exclamatory statement, or try for a combination of several objectives.)

**Students sometimes will ask if they can add bats to the bat box. Some of the best writing will come from their ideas.

3-10 NOVEMBER—STORY STARTERS (4-6)

Objective: After this activity the student should be able to complete a creative essay using the given starter sentences or themes.

Materials Needed:

- chief for bulletin board
- pencils
- thumbtacks

- copies of feather pattern with story starters written on them

Procedure:

1. Mount the "bald" Indian chief on the bulletin board or center. Copy the following story starters on the feathers and let the children add them to the headdress as each student completes a creative writing essay.

Story Starters:

— I was the only one left...

— The Legend of the Purple Pumpkin

— Alone in the mountains, I suddenly turned and...

— Running Cloud was the only brave who had a chance at...

— Make a recipe booklet for a unique Thanksgiving feast. Omit turkey, ham, and sweet potatoes.

— Design a practical use for turkey feathers.

— Combine Thanksgiving and Veteran's Day. How would you celebrate the new day. What would you call the new day?

— Peter, the Pilgrim, was concerned. He was in charge of...

2. Allow your students to come up with their own "story-starter" feathers.

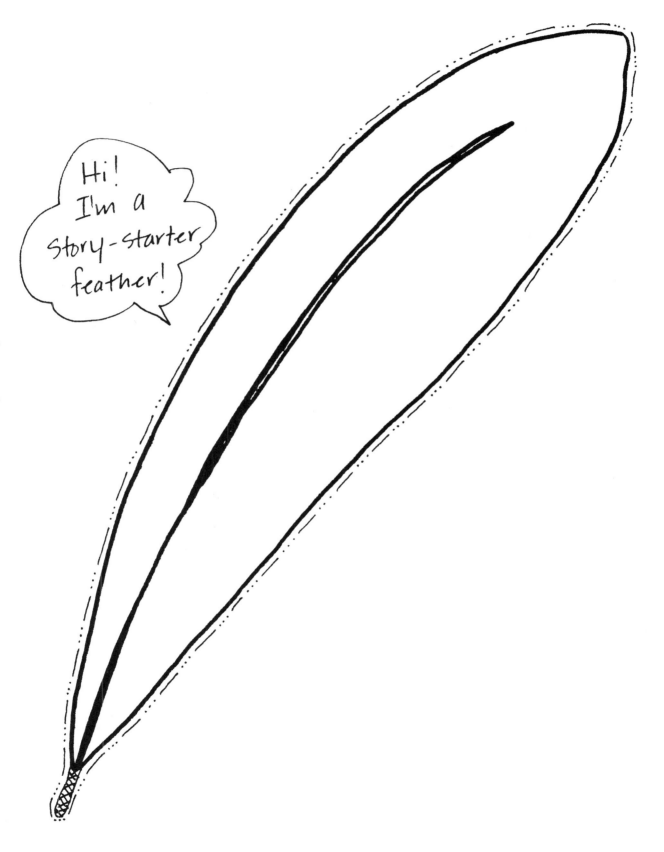

3-11 DECEMBER—WHAT'S IN A CARD? (4-6)

Objective: After this activity the student should be able to incorporate the given holiday theme into a creative essay.

Materials Needed:

- old Christmas and Hanukkah cards
- paper
- pencils

Procedure:

1. With many different religious celebrations in the month of December, it is probably to the benefit of the class to incorporate many ideas in writing. At the end of November ask the class to bring in old Christmas cards and Hanukkah cards.

2. Use the following creative writing ideas in the cards, then place the writing on the bulletin board while the cards are surrounding the board.

Writing Ideas:

— I was a burned out light bulb.

— I was the only green blinking light on the tree.

— I was an identical twin snowflake. I had to find my brother or sister soon.

— Make a list of concrete and abstract gifts you might give to someone 70 years old.

— The unicorn wants to be part of the symbolism of this season. Decide if you would like him to join the symbols. List reasons for or against his application.

— Visiting is done during this season. Choose someone you'd like to visit and write down the things you'd like to talk about (a famous, living, or nonliving person is acceptable).

— Design a set of four cards to get across the seasonal message. They may be serious or amusing. Select an original character to be in the main theme.

3. Tell the students beforehand that you will be looking into "originality" during this month. Discuss the term, permit them to give examples before writing starts.

3-12 SPRING IN JANUARY (4-6)

Objective: After completing this activity the student should be able to brainstorm ideas on the given theme and generate new ideas.

Procedure:

1. The universal theme for January seems to be snow and snowmen so let's change the usual. Make this "Spring in January." Have the students brainstorm all the usual spring words and write them on the board.

2. Then tell the students to combine thoughts they've brainstormed and come up with a new holiday celebrating the best of the two seasons.

3. You may want to divide them into groups or have them work individually. Students love this activity and it adds a little something to the drab winter doldrums!

Ideas for Challenge:

    — Name could be Spruary, or Janing

    — What kinds of flowers could be added?

    — Another use for snow

    — How to make a Sandman

    — Tools for cutting grass

3-13 FEBRUARY—VALID VALENTINES (4-6)

Objective: After completing this activity the student should be able to write an expressive essay on the Valentine theme.

Materials Needed:

- large Valentine candy box
- paper hearts
- paper
- pencils

Procedure:

Use an empty Valentine box (heart-shaped) in the center. On hearts inside the candy box, print the following:

— How lonely it is to…

— My first broken heart

— Ode to a Valentine

— Change the day to October 1. What types of problems or interesting situations would the change make?

— Research the beginning of Valentine's Day. What was the reasoning behind this celebration?

— Design a new Valentine using any color except red, pink, and white. Write a commercial to hook your classmates into this new Valentine.

— Design a bumper sticker to express your feelings. It must be short, make a good statement, relate to Valentine's Day, and be attractive. You may want to submit several to a class committee and get their opinion. Then, design five for adults to place on their cars.

3-14 MARCH—SOARING IDEAS (4-6)

Objective: After completing this activity the student should be able to write an expressive essay on the given topic.

Materials Needed:

- napkins
- cloth squares

Procedure:

1. Use colorful, inexpensive napkins for kites. Many one-of-a-kind napkins can be purchased from linen stores which just want to get rid of them. Ask if they could be donated to the school. Students can raid mom's sewing baskets for scraps. Story starters can be placed on the tails of kites.
2. Place finished writing on the kites.

Ideas for starters:

— Leo the Lion and Lammie the Lamb weren't exactly the best of friends...

— Compare the saying "March comes in like a lion and goes out like a lamb" to "Old soldiers never die, they just fade away."

— What are the "ides of March"?

— Save your straws from the lunchroom and then design a kite. Assemble the straws and kite, make a tail, and see if it will fly. Why? Why not?

— Research St. Patrick. Why is he important?

— Compare the gremlins with the leprechauns.

— Make a leprechaun out of clay. Give him a name. Write about his adventure before you "captured" him.

— Analyze the reasons why the lion and the lamb are used in this month. Select two other animals which you think may be a better choice.

— Design a unique weather vane for the class. Mount it on the outside of the window and keep reading of wind direction for a week.

3-15 APRIL—CRACK ME OPEN (4-6)

Objective: After completing this activity, the student should be able to write a creative essay on the given topic.

Materials Needed:

- basket
- straw for basket
- plastic eggs
- paper
- pencils

Procedure:

1. Ask a student to bring in an old basket.
2. Collect plastic eggs and place the following story starters in the eggs. Students like opening the eggs. There should be one strip which will say "FREE." If a student chooses that one, he or she may write about anything desired. It does not have to pertain to the month's theme.

Story Starters:

— Freddy the rabbit had a major problem to solve. He found out that...

— Write a new spring song which will tell about spring smells. It may be amusing or serious. Combine the lyrics with music.

— Cleo was an unusual rabbit. She couldn't hop.

— Mr. Rabbit has decided to retire. He doesn't want another rabbit to take his place, so we must think of a different animal to deliver Easter eggs to the children. Justify your choice of animal. List the advantages and disadvantages of your choice.

— FREE

— The Rabbit Council thinks America should take a serious look at the use of a rabbit's foot as a good luck piece. Submit a letter to the Council explaining to them your idea for a change.

— Compare the use of the symbol of the rabbit for this month with the lion or the lamb from last month. Why do we use animals as symbols?

3-16 MAY—BLOOMING IDEAS (4-6)

Objective: After completing this activity the student should be able to write a creative essay on the given topic.

Materials Needed:

- construction paper in various colors
- scissors
- pencils

Procedure:

1. Have the students make large flowers and use them for a border to go around the bulletin board or center.
2. You may want to have the students write story starters on the stems.

Story Starters:

— I am an unusual flower. My father was a day lily and my mother was a rose. Can you imagine how peculiar I look? How out of place I am!

— I am a weed and I'm tired of getting no appreciation.

— There are many unusual wild flowers in the world. Use the Wild Flower Guide and research any three. Draw these three real wild flowers on a poster with two you make up. Make sure each has a short paragraph mentioning its name, any fact which seems different, and where it is located. Place your poster on the bulletin board for others to guess which ones are the real wild flowers.

— Make up a commercial about Spring. What could you say to make people buy some Spring?

— Make a booklet with three to five poems about Spring which would be suitable for the K-1 age. Have students share these booklets with the K-1 classes at the end of the month.

— Design a "teacher" flower. Anything goes!

3-17 JUNE—CREATIVE WRITING PLUG-INS (4-6)

Below are listed ideas that may be used in June or just as a change from the seasonal ones.

1. Announce to the class that today is "Pig Day." Everything will deal with pigs.

   a. The science class will research pigs, their uses, the different varieties of pigs, and the anatomy of pigs. (Perhaps a spokesman from a college or a local farmer could speak with the class.)
   b. Language class could experience Pig Latin. (Pig Latin is spoken by removing the first letter of a word, placing it at the end, and adding an A. For example, boy becomes oybā; jokes changes to okesjā.)
   c. Writing class could write just about pigs' adventures. Some students will want to use the Pig Latin. How about Pig Limericks?
   d. Social Studies could find out where in the United States most pigs are raised. Ask the students to suggest why so many pigs are raised in a particular area. What do pigs eat?
   e. Math class could make up word problems about pigs and their problems.
   f. Have a lunch treat of "pigs in a blanket" or "pork 'n beans."

2. The same could be done for any animal or vegetable—Peanut Day, Carrot Day, Elephant Day.

3. Have a list of children's nursery rhymes. Ask the students to change the rhymes to fit another purpose—Halloween, Dog Days, Spring, Smile Day.

4. Get an old suitcase and place different objects in it. Have students, without looking, pull out an object. They may not change objects. Have them write about the object travelling with them, getting lost, belonging to someone else, or from the perspective of how an ant or elephant would see this object.

5. Interpretation is a difficult skill for this age. Try a few short phrases for the students:

   a. A stitch in time saves nine.

   b. A sharp tongue is the only edged tool that grows keener with constant use.

   c. Listen more with the heart than the mind.

   d. A narrow mind becomes a stubborn mind.

   e. The reward of a thing well done is to have done it.

   f. There is no traffic jam on the "extra mile."

3-18 PARTS OF SPEECH FILE FUN (4-6)

Objective: After completing this activity, the student should be able to identify the different parts of speech.

Materials Needed:

- 3″ × 5″ colored note cards made from construction paper
- 11″ × 17″ construction paper
- markers or crayons
- stapler
- scissors

Procedure

1. Parts of speech are relatively easy to define. However, using them correctly in their own writing presents many problems for the intermediate grade child. So we'll set the study up as a business. Tell the students, "We are going to study the different parts of speech as a business. What does one need in a business?" The students will begin to list items needed in a business: store, cash register, money, different items on a shelf.

Table
Chair
Office
Typewriter
Paper

File Cabinets
Bank account
Business cards
Telephone
Pens

   Most of the things listed in this brainstorming session will be nouns. Separate them out and have students write them on *green* cards. Perhaps they could find pictures to go with the nouns. Choose one of the nouns and ask, "What can we do to this?" Example: money—spend, borrow, steal, add, subtract. Have a student write these words on *red* cards.

2. Continue with:

   Adjectives— "What words could we use to describe— money?" (Example: green, old, wrinkled, torn. Write these on *blue* cards.)

   Adverbs— "What words would be used to modify the adjectives?" (very, advantageously, currently, naturally—on *pink* cards)

   Prepositional phrases— "Where could you put the money?" (in a box, around the house, on the piano, beside the desk—on *purple* cards)

   Interjections— "What words could be used to describe how you feel when you spend money?" (great, wow, terrific, yea—on *yellow* cards)

Conjunctions—"What words would you use to combine any of the ideas?" (and, but, or, either/or, neither/nor—on *orange* cards)

3. Assign dollar amounts to certain cards. See who can make the most expensive sentence using all parts of speech. The students will get so excited they will begin to ask if they can add other words to the different colored cards. Suggest they consult a dictionary for identifying words with more than one usage. Keep a log noting the dollar amounts each child earns. Challenge them to beat their own records. Set aside a time frame for playing "Business" every Friday.

4. After your students have compiled a long list of words, have the students copy the list. Now your students will label each of the words on the list. Label each one either a noun, pronoun, verb, adjective, adverb, preposition, conjunction, or interjection.

5. *Making the "Parts of Speech File"*: Guide and direct your students to make a folder using eight pieces of colored 11" × 17" construction paper.

   — First fold each piece of paper in half

   — Label each with a different category: Noun, Verb, Preposition, Pronoun, Adjective, Adverb, Conjunction, and Interjection. Cut tabs in the eight sheets so that they resemble file folders.

   — Staple the pages together at the bottom and one side. Leave the top and one side open. The students will store various lists and other assignments in these individual folders.

6. *Verbs*: What do we do with our verbs? Pull one of the brainstorm words out. "What can we do to a *table*?" Most words will be *verbs*. Copy a list from the board and place in the verb folder.

7. *Nouns/Verbs*: Have students pull out nouns and verbs, cut them apart and place to make beginning sentences. What's missing?

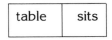

table	sits

Noun markers—*This* table sits.

Add all noun markers to folder under "Nouns."

8. *Adjectives*: What can we say about the *folder*? Torn, red, musty, etc. Add these words to sample sentence structures.

9. *Adverb*: Set up a sentence. For example:

The dirty, green table sits <u>How?</u>

Make a list. Brainstorm with your students to come up with various adverbs.

10. *Pronoun*: Pull out the list of nouns. What can be used for:

students—we, us, I, you, she, he

folder—it

Put these in the pronoun section.

11. *Prepositions:* Where can you place the folder?

on the table	*between*
in the desk	*around*
on top of	*among*
inside	*up*
beside	*down*

Have students write out phrases to add to the folder. Place these in the "Preposition" folder.

12. *Conjunction:* What would be connectors between "students" and "folders"?

and	but
nor	or

Add to these folders.

13. *Interjections*: The principal has stopped our business. What can we say? "…Oh, no!" "Rats!" "Darn!"

RESEARCH TOPICS FOR FURTHER STUDY OF "WRITING WISELY"

Presented here are a collection of research topics for the exploring mind. The topics are designed to encourage divergent as well as convergent thinking. *Beware:* young researchers may end up detouring into uncharted waters of knowledge and discovery. Encourage and welcome these departures.

1. Compose a "parts of speech" rock jingle. Record the jingle.

2. Develop a dramatic production with characters being the parts of speech.

3. Write the narration for a film about an important event at your school. Videotape the event. Record the narration so that it can accompany the film.

4. Cut and paste phrases and pictures from magazines and newspapers to fashion a poem which expresses a strong feeling you had that week.

5. Compare and contrast the written format of two national magazines. Develop a student magazine which embodies the best of both magazines.

6. Research the presentation styles of four cereal commercials. Identify the strengths and weaknesses of each commercial. Are they successful in persuading you of their worth? Summarize what appear to be their techniques of persuasion. Develop a written summary.

7. Study the amount of time allotted to one commercial. Investigate how much of the time is verbal in content? How much of the time is pictorial? Compose a written summary of your results.

8. Conduct an analysis of the verbal content of one commercial. How much of what is said is factual? Nonfactual? Share your results.

9. Cut beige cotton cloth into 8″ × 8″ squares. Using cloth paint, have students paint the parts of speech on the squares. Then sew the squares together to make a skirt, apron, or quilted wall hanging.

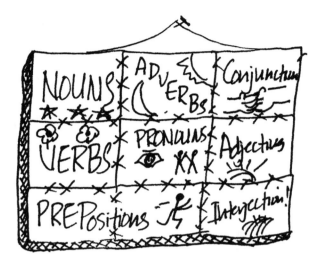

10. Have students write a play using only the parts of speech as characters. Make this a videotape.

11. Write an evaluation of the students' business using words developed in the folder.

12. Develop a song with verses telling about the different parts of speech.

13. Have students bring in old T-shirts. Using cloth pens, ask students to write all the words in their folder under correct headings on their T-shirt or design a full sentence on the back. Or, create their own motto, saying, or value statement using a pun.

14. Set up a court case on a part of speech being misused. For example:

> Eight jurors each representing the eight parts of speech—Mr. Con Junction, Ms. Noun; Mr. I. R. Verb, Ms. Ima Adjective, Mr. C. M. Adverb, Ms. Inter Jection, Mr. In Preposition.
>
> Judge—All Words Justice
>
> Prosecuting attorney—Mr. I. M. Right
>
> Defense attorney—Mr. U. R. Wrong
>
> Defendant—Ms. Ura Noun

Have a list of words which can be *used* in different ways. Example: run, trust, badger, dodge, miss, etc. Read to the judge and jury sentences—for example:

"I *run* twenty miles a week to keep in shape."

"The *run* was terribly tiring."

"I *trust* the coach to give a straight answer."

"A *trust* fund is for my sick aunt."

"The *trust* one expects from a friend is great."

"She constantly *badgers* the rest of the group."

"A *badger* named Ginger was the hit of the play."

"I *miss* not seeing you often."

"The *missed* friend soon returned to the chorus."

Have Ms. Ura Noun represent all the words as nouns. Let the jury decide if she is guilty. Capable students will be able to convince a jury to return a not-guilty verdict, at times.

Students enjoy finding out about words which can be used differently. They will soon be able to add their own.

BIBLIOGRAPHY FOR "WRITING WISELY"

Center Stuff for Nooks, Crannies, and Corners by Imogene Forte, Mary Ann Pangle and Robbie Tupa (Nashville, TN: Incentive Publications, 1973).

The Reading Corner: Ideas, Games and Activities for Individualizing Reading by Harry W. Forgan (Santa Monica, CA: Goodyear Publishing Company, 1977).

Creative Writing in Action by Elizabeth Marten and Nina Crosby (Carthage, IL: Good Apple, Inc., 1981).

Ideas for Teachers from Teachers (Urbana, IL: National Council of Teachers of English, 1983).

If You're Trying to Teach Kids How to Write, You've Gotta Have This Book! by Marjorie Frank (Nashville, TN: Incentive Publications, 1979).

Writing Corner by Arnold B. Cheyney (Santa Monica, CA: Goodyear Publishing Company, 1979).

Section 4

RESEARCH ROUNDUP

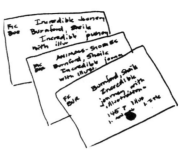

    This chapter will give students a firm footing in the fundamentals of doing research in the school or community library. They will gain a better understanding of the Dewey Decimal classification system, acquire new appreciation for autobiographies as important sources of information, develop a working knowledge of the card catalog system, and learn how to effectively use dictionaries. Imagine participating in a "Dewey Lottery."

ACTIVITY TITLE AND GRADE LEVEL	SKILLS USED
Do We Know Dewey?	
4-1 Class Feet (K-3)	classifying; hypothesizing
4-2 Who Needs It? (K-3)	collecting data; comparing; classifying
4-3 The Whole Is the Sum of Its Parts (K-3)	interpreting; comparing
4-4 Scavenger Hunt (K-3)	collecting and organizing data
4-5 Match-U (K-3)	comparing
4-6 Betcha' Know or Dewey Lottery (K-3)	looking for assumptions; hypothesizing; collecting and organizing data
4-7 Dramatized Dewey (4-6)	hypothesizing; problem solving
4-8 Make-A-Monster (4-6)	collecting data

ACTIVITY TITLE AND GRADE LEVEL   SKILLS USED

The Hidden History of Heroes

4-9	Heroes in Our Midst (4-6)	comparing; collecting and organizing data
4-10	The Provocative Question (4-6)	problem solving; imagining; collecting data
4-11	Setting Up the Interview (4-6)	organizing data
4-12	The Interview (4-6)	collecting data
4-13	Production Time (4-6)	classifying; summarizing; organizing data
4-14	Collective Biography (4-6)	organizing data

Playing Your Cards...Right!

4-15	Anatomy of a Card (4-6)	criticizing; observing; classifying
4-16	One Equals Three (4-6)	interpreting; criticizing
4-17	Number Pull-Eeze (4-6)	collecting and organizing data; looking for assumptions
4-18	Copy Cats! (4-6)	collecting and organizing data
4-19	Create a Card (4-6)	organizing data; criticizing

ACTIVITY TITLE AND GRADE LEVEL	SKILLS USED
Dictionary Delight	
4-20 The "Guide"-ing Light (4-6)	coding; observing
4-21 "Guide" to Math (4-6)	organizing data
4-22 Two-Clue-Teasers (4-6)	organizing data
4-23 A Nu Lang'-Gwij (4-6)	observing; criticizing
4-24 Help the Turkey Trot (4-6)	coding; interpreting; problem solving
4-25 In Other Words (4-6)	comparing; collecting data

Topics for Further Study

Bibliography

Do We Know Dewey?

A better understanding of the Dewey Decimal Classification system can reap many rewards for the budding young researcher. The following activities will unlock the doors of the library for your students.

4-1 CLASS FEET (K-3)

Objective: After completing this activity the student should be able to explain the uses of a classification system.

Materials Needed:

- shoes that children are wearing
- dictionary at the level of class

Procedure:

1. Begin by defining the word "classification." Have a pair of children locate the word in the dictionary provided and read the definition. Explain that large numbers of items are more easily located if they are sorted and classified.

2. Have each child remove both his or her shoes. These will be placed in two distinct piles. (One student could collect left shoes, another student, right shoes.) Divide the group in half and explain that each group, working with their own pile of shoes, will be given 10 to 15 minutes to sort them and classify them as they please. If groups are having problems, clues may be given...girls' shoes, boys' shoes, leather shoes, plastic shoes, brown shoes, tennis shoes, etc.

3. At the end of the allotted time, the groups may select a spokesperson to explain his or her group's system. (Could they arrange their shoes at home

using this method?) Finish by asking students to think about other large numbers of things which could be classified. Name a few.

4-2 WHO NEEDS IT? (K-3)

Objective: After completing this activity students should be able to discuss how classification is important in a library.

Materials Needed:

- posterboard
- magic marker

- large photograph of Dewey shown here

Procedure:

1. Position the posterboard so that all may see. Begin by listing (or having children list) things which could be classified to be better understood and more accessible. Hopefully, they should suggest several items like these:

   - department stores
   - grocery stores
   - plants
   - animals
   - stamps
   - rocks
   - dolls
   - and...books!

2. Leave space next to what is listed for mentioning some possible methods of classification. (Example: In the "Department Store," items could be classified by size, shape, color, materials, where used, etc.)

3. Show the class the photograph of Melvil Dewey as you give a short biographical sketch of the man. (You might prefer a transparency, easily made from a copy of the illustration and a thermal transparency.) Especially mention that he developed his system of classification in 1876 and it is still used today in most smaller libraries. Point out the benefits of becoming familiar with the Dewey system of classification. If you know, for example, that fairy tales are located in 398.2, then you know exactly where to head in each new library to find fairy tales.

MELVIL DEWEY

4-3 THE WHOLE IS THE SUM OF ITS PARTS (K-3)

Objective: After completing this activity the student should be able to describe how numerals are important to topics in a library.

Materials Needed:

- transparency of the ten Dewey decimal areas
- transparency of the 700s, broken down into major parts
- transparency of the 796s, broken down further

Procedure:

1. Make the three transparencies. As transparency 1 is shown, reveal only one level at a time as the explanation is given. (Show several books from that level before proceeding, if need be.)

2. Using the 700s as an example, explain how this section is divided and what kinds of subjects are included. Then choose several students. Give each a different 700 number. Some good ones might be: 709, 784, 791, 745. Have them go to the shelves and determine what kind of book is found at that location. (They may bring one book back as an example.) After they share their findings, compare results with transparency 2.

3. Finally, explain that Dewey wanted to be very specific in order to help us. Show the last transparency and decide what types of books belong in this subdivision.

THE DEWEY CLASSIFICATION SYSTEM

000-099 General Works
100-199 Philosophy
200-299 Religion
300-399 Social Sciences
400-499 Language
500-599 Pure Science
600-699 Technology
700-799 The Arts
800-899 Literature
900-999 History

Here is the way some people like to remember the broad outline of the system.

When primitive man learned to think, his first thoughts were about himself and the people around him (100—Psychology and Personality).

He attributed the things he could not understand to a Supreme Being and religion began (200—Religion).

Families became groups and groups became communities. It was necessary to live in harmony with others (300—Social Science).

People had to communicate with each other and invented speech (400—Language).

As he developed, man began to wonder about the world around him (500—Pure Science).

He made life easier for himself when he put to use some of the knowledge he acquired (600—Technology).

He now found time for recreation, painting, music (700—Fine Arts).

In order that others might profit from his experiences, he put them in writing (800—Literature).

He left behind him a record of his achievements (900—History).

Transparency 2

700s
700—The Arts, Fine and Decorative Arts
710—Civic and Landscape Art
720—Architecture
730—Plastic Arts Sculpture
740—Drawing, and Decorative, and Minor Arts
750—Painting and Paintings
760—Graphic Arts, Print Making, and Prints
770—Photography
780—Music
790—Recreational and Performing Arts

Transparency 3

796	Athletic and Outdoor Sports
796.3	Ball Games
796.31	Ball Thrown or Hit By Hand
796.33	Ball Driven By Foot
796.34	Racquet Games
796.35	Ball Driven By Club, Mallet, Bat
796.352	Golf
796.357	Baseball

4-4 SCAVENGER HUNT (K-3)

Objective: After completing this activity the student should be able to locate topics using the Dewey Decimal system.

Materials Needed:

- four to six lists of items, subjects in Media Center for groups to locate using knowledge of Dewey Decimal System

- copies of Media Center coupons for winning group (good for 30 minutes free time in Media Center, at teacher's discretion)
- paper
- pencils

Procedure:

1. Explain that the class will be divided into groups. Each group will be given a list of things to locate. Answers must be written on their papers to qualify. The time limit will be 15 to 20 minutes. Excessive noise will mean that a group may be disqualified. The winning group will receive a prize. See the illustration for sample questions/items. Obviously, lists must be designed for use in your Media Center and involve only media found there.

2. At the end of the allotted time, groups are asked to stop. If no group has finished, the group with the most answers surrenders its list for class perusal. If answers are correct, coupons are awarded.

Suggestion: Encourage children to work efficiently as a group—sharing responsibilities and dividing labor.

Find answers to the following: Group's Name _____

1. Biographies have what Dewey number?

2. Where would you find books that tell you how to make things?

3. What's the difference between 597 and 599?

4. What kind of book fills more than half the shelves in the 300s?

5. Which come first…religious books or language books?

6. Where are travel books?

7. What author writes many books on the solar system?

8. What kind of book is found in 817?

9. Where are magic books?

10. What two locations can you give for joke/riddle books?

11. In 641 are books we need daily. What are they?

12. Give the name of one author who has written many fairy tales?

13. Do "human body" books come before or after "animal" books?

14. Are call numbers for biographies all the same? If not, how are they different?

Copy these coupons... for your students!

MEDIA CENTER COUPON

ADMIT ONE Name: _____
Teacher: _____
Redeemable at time approved by teacher

THIS COUPON ENTITLES THE BEARER TO ONE 30-MINUTE-TIME IN THE MEDIA CENTER FOR USE AS BEARER DESIRES.

Appropriate uses include: Filmstrip viewing, listening to tapes (audio/video), reading, or finishing homework.

MEDIA CENTER COUPON

ADMIT ONE Name: _____
Teacher: _____
Redeemable at time approved by teacher

THIS COUPON ENTITLES THE BEARER TO ONE 30-MINUTE-TIME IN THE MEDIA CENTER FOR USE AS BEARER DESIRES.

Appropriate uses include: Filmstrip viewing, listening to tapes (audio/video), reading, or finishing homework.

MEDIA CENTER COUPON

ADMIT ONE Name: _____
Teacher: _____
Redeemable at time approved by teacher

THIS COUPON ENTITLES THE BEARER TO ONE 30-MINUTE-TIME IN THE MEDIA CENTER FOR USE AS BEARER DESIRES.

Appropriate uses include: Filmstrip viewing, listening to tapes (audio/video), reading, or finishing homework.

4-5 MATCH-U (K-3)

Objective: After completing this activity the student should be able to relate topics to Dewey Decimal numerals.

Materials Needed:

- materials for making spinner (see instructions sheet)

- materials for making playing cards (see instructions sheet)

Procedure:

1. This is a matching game to reinforce students' understanding of the Dewey Decimal System. The game is designed for four players.

2. One player deals the 20 cards face down, one to a player until all have been dealt. Players may examine their cards.

3. The first player spins the spinner and announces where it stops. At that time, any player who can "match" his subject or title to the classification area lays down that card. This player also becomes the next person to spin.

4. The object of the game is to play all cards first and "go out."

5. *Suggestions*: Some students will want to jump up, run to the shelves or card catalog, and verify. Many groups could not handle this much activity. Please consider your group and restrict the activity accordingly.

If a spinner is not available, you may use dice remembering that "11" and "12" would have to be re-rolled. In all cases, convert the numbers into a hundred level (Example: 3 = 300s).

SPINNER INSTRUCTIONS SHEET

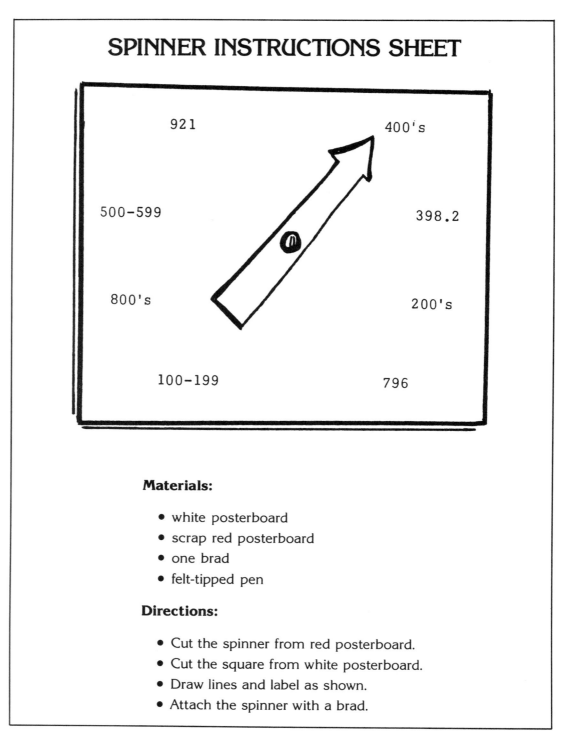

Materials:

- white posterboard
- scrap red posterboard
- one brad
- felt-tipped pen

Directions:

- Cut the spinner from red posterboard.
- Cut the square from white posterboard.
- Draw lines and label as shown.
- Attach the spinner with a brad.

PLAYING CARDS INSTRUCTIONS

Materials:

- 20 3″ × 4″ rectangles of yellow posterboard
- fine-tip black marker

Directions:

- On each of the 20 cards, write *one* of the following...

The Golden Fleece	*¿Eres tu mi mama?*
plays	*Great Religions of the World*
jogging	*Ghosts of the Carolinas*
Ghost Poems	mythology
Hailstones and Halibut Bones	*Strega Nona*
Daniel Boone	*Little Red Riding Hood*
presidents	sign language
Insect Pets	feelings—happy, mad, etc.
Poor Richard in France	dictionaries
Run or Pass	snakes

FEEL FREE TO ADD YOUR OWN!

4-6 BETCHA' KNOW or DEWEY LOTTERY (K-3)

Objective: After completing this activity the student should be able to predict a Dewey Decimal numeral.

Materials Needed:

- shoe box with lid (bearing slot for guessing)
- slips of paper on which to record guesses
- pencils
- posterboard for displaying directions
- three books, new (purchased) or newly received (donated by family or P.T.A.)

Procedure:

1. Find a prominent spot in the Media Center for this exciting display. This is your own Dewey Lottery to review and enhance learning of the Dewey Decimal System.

2. A posterboard with directions should explain to students:

   — This is a lottery (you may cast your votes).
   — Look at three books on display...Do not remove jackets, however.
   — Write down each title and *what you think* is the appropriate Dewey number.
   — Fold the paper with the guesses and put it in the slot of the box.
   — Write your name and home room.

3. Books should be covered with non-transparent covers. If Dewey number is written *anywhere* in book, it should be concealed.

4. Children should look at books, follow instructions, record guesses, and put them in the box. Winners' names will be announced the following week.

4-7 DRAMATIZED DEWEY (4-6)

Objective: After completing this activity the student should be able to dramatize a Dewey Decimal classification area.

Materials Needed: • none

Procedure:

1. The class is divided into small groups of three to six people. Each group will have ten minutes to: (1) choose a Dewey Decimal classification area, (2) decide how to pantomime or enact it, and (3) gather any necessary props.

Then, one by one, the groups will perform while the remainder of the class attempts to guess which Dewey area and/or which number is being presented.

2. Suggestion:

— Try to stick to time limit as time will pass rapidly when groups are performing.

— Performances may be videotaped in order to be enjoyed at a later date.

4-8 MAKE-A-MONSTER (4-6)

Objective: After completing this activity the student should be able to read works from various Dewey Decimal topic areas.

Materials Needed:

- copies of monster's body parts
- different colors of construction paper
- brads

Procedure:

1. Each time a child reads from a different Dewey level, another monster body part is awarded until child has read from all ten divisions and has received all the monster parts.

2. Completed monsters could then be assembled in classrooms or in Media Center for all to see.

3. This should serve as a good reading incentive program, as well as a culminating activity on the Dewey Decimal System of Classification.

4. Suggestions:

— Body parts could be run off on different colors of construction paper to make the monster more interesting.

— Body part numbers could coincide with hundred levels of Dewey (*Example*: Book read from 200s—student receives part 2, etc.)

— Parent volunteers would be helpful in the awarding of monster parts as the books are returned.

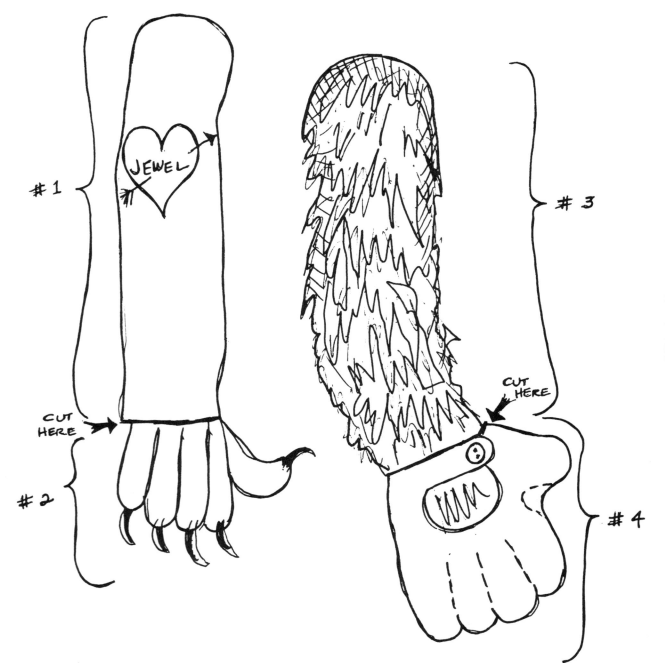

#1

JEWEL

CUT
HERE

#2

#3

CUT
HERE

#4

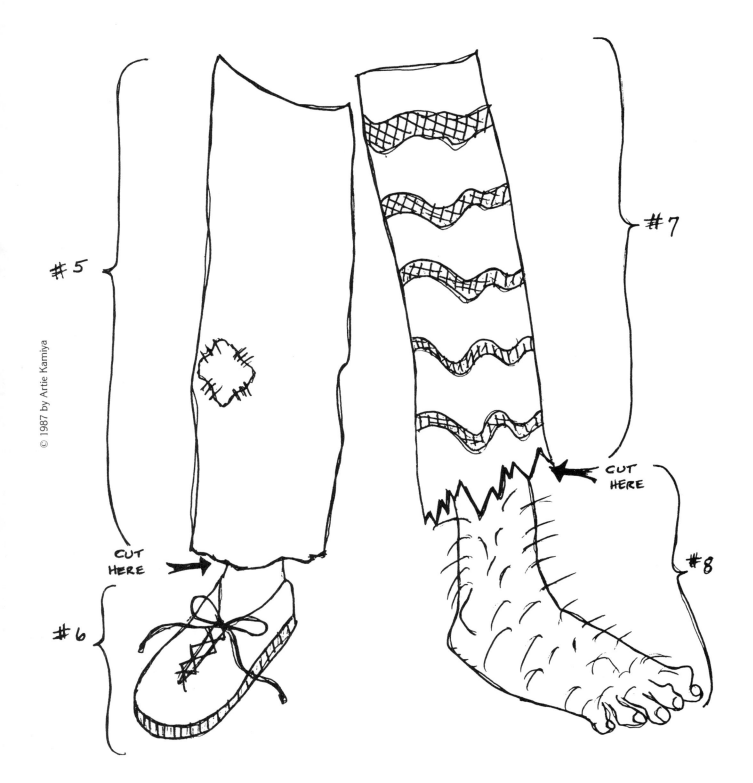

#5

#7

© 1987 by Artie Kamiya

CUT
HERE →

#6

CUT
← HERE

#8

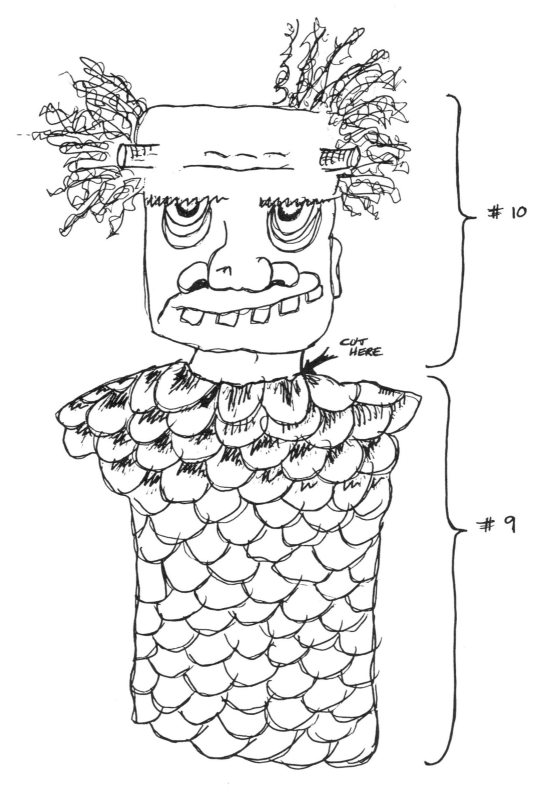

CUT
HERE

10

9

The Hidden History of Heroes

Biographies and autobiographies are an important resource when doing research. The hidden history of heroes can be uncovered, giving depth and personality to a research project. The following exciting activities give the gifted and talented student an excellent introduction to biographies and autobiographies.

4-9 HEROES IN OUR MIDST (4-6)

Objective: After completing this activity the student should be able to compose a simple biographical and autobiographical statement.

Materials Needed:

- several biographies by one author
- an autobiography

- copies of personal shields
- extra writing paper
- pencils

Procedure:

1. What is a biography? What is an autobiography? Let's find out! Ask your students to find a partner.
2. Each partner should complete the unfinished sentences of the "Personal Shield."
3. Once the "Personal Shields" are completed, ask partners to share their "Personal Shields." Make sure to allow enough time for sharing. Each student should then be given an 8½" × 11" sheet of writing paper which students are to fold in half lengthwise. On the upper half students should write a paragraph about their partner. On the lower half, students should write a paragraph summarizing special and unique qualities about them-

PERSONAL SHIELD

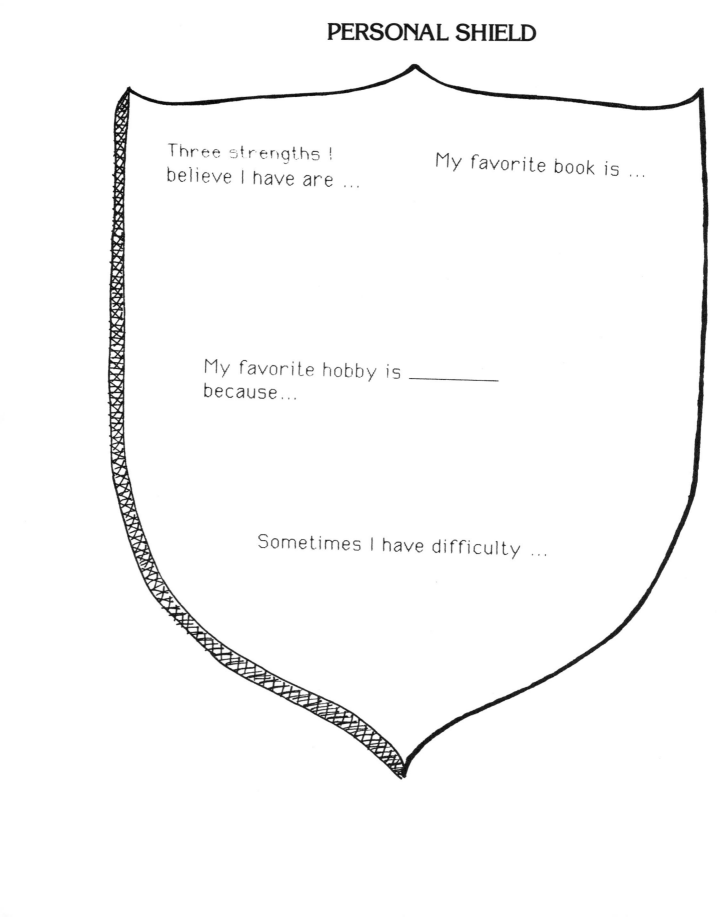

Three strengths I believe I have are ...

My favorite book is ...

My favorite hobby is _____ because...

Sometimes I have difficulty ...

selves. These summaries are examples of biographies and autobiographies. How are they different? How are they the same? After discussion, volunteers could share their "Personal Shields" with the rest of the class.

4. Review the concepts of biography and autobiography after shields have been shared. Remind students that not just "famous" persons are included in biographies/autobiographies. Also point out that persons do not have to be deceased to be the subject of a biography/autobiography.

5. Conclude by mentioning that the examination of the call number will reveal three letters which refer to the "person" described in the biography, not the author's last name. This is a fact unique to biographies.

4-10 THE PROVOCATIVE QUESTION (4-6)

Objective: After completing this activity the student should be able to develop a list of interview questions.

Materials Needed:

- chalkboard or large sheet of newsprint
- magic marker

Procedure:

1. Biographies are written about interesting, remarkable, and unusual things in a person's life. Why? Because the biographies are more exciting to read.

2. Imagine that a publishing company has asked your firm, "Creative Biographies," to compile biographies of special people in your school.

3. Before conducting interviews, a list of ten provocative questions must be compiled by "Creative Biographies." These provocative questions will be used during interviews with important school personalities. You may want to read some tips about provocative questions before generating a list.

4. *Suggestions*: Avoid yes/no questions like the plague. Beginning a question with "how" or "what" will get you off to a good start. Think about the unusual. Imaginative "if" questions can elicit exciting information also. *Example*: "If you were an eagle, how would *you* do your job differently?"

Now develop a list of at least ten provocative questions to be used in the interviews.

4-11 SETTING UP THE INTERVIEW (4-6)

Objective: After completing this activity the student should have made an appointment with an important school personality.

Materials Needed:

- None

Procedure:

1. Each interview team should select an important school personality (principal, physical education teacher, custodian) to interview.
2. Each team should meet with their important school personality and accomplish the following:

    — Smile

    — Introduce yourselves

    — Explain that you wish to conduct a taped interview and would like to set up an appointment for the interview

    — Thank the school personality

4-12 THE INTERVIEW (4-6)

Objective: After completing this activity the student should be able to conduct an interview.

Materials Needed:

- one cassette recorder for each two interviewers
- one empty cassette for each interviewing team

Procedure:

1. "Creative Biographies" is now ready to interview. Remember those provocative questions!
2. Suggest that the interview team arrive a few minutes before the scheduled interview. Their questions should be written and ready. It also is a good idea to have used the cassette recorder beforehand.
3. One student can be responsible for recording the interview on cassette while the partner asks the questions. Remember to thank the interviewee for his or her time.

4-13 PRODUCTION TIME (4-6)

Objective: After completing this activity the student should be able to organize the results of an interview into a written format.

Materials Needed:

- several pairs of scissors
- black magic marker
- stapler

Procedure:

1. Ask interview teams to review their taped interviews. After listening to the complete interview, partners should decide what were the exciting or unusual aspects of the interview.
2. The interviews should then be written up as short biographies with special attention given to any unusual information.
3. These biographies can be bound using construction paper and a stapler.

4. Demonstrate how the call number could be placed close to the spine. Remember, individual biographies always have a B or 921 followed by the first three letters of the person's (interviewee) last name.

Example: Call number for principal Ms. Long

```
921
Lon
```

4-14 COLLECTIVE BIOGRAPHY (4-6)

Objective: After completing this activity the student should be able to find a collective biography in their school media center.

Materials Needed: • one binder

Procedure:

1. The publishing company is excited about the school biographies and would like them to be published as a collective biography. The call number will need to be changed from 921 to 920. Also, the first three letters should be of the author's last name. "Creative Biographies" (the students) should bind the individual biographies into a collective biography using a binder.

2. Don't forget to add the call number on the spine. A copy of the collective biographies should be added to the school media center collection and kept on card file. This has been another success story for the "Creative Biographies" firm. Good job!

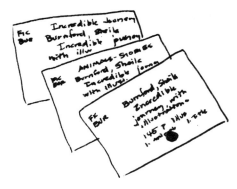

Playing Your Cards... Right!

Finding what you want in the school media center or community library is both challenging and rewarding. The following activities will catapult your students onward as they strive to gather diverse sources for their research projects.

4-15 ANATOMY OF A CARD (4-6)

Objective: After completing this activity the student should be able to identify parts of a card catalog.

Materials Needed:

- enlargement of labeled "Card Anatomy" sheet
- transparency of same catalog card, unlabeled
- pencils
- paper
- laminated catalog cards

Procedure:

1. Since children have varying levels of knowledge regarding the card catalog, it's best to call this first part an *overview* or *review* before "we play a game."

2. Explain that the card catalog is our "index" for media found in our Media Center. Each book, record, and filmstrip has three card catalog cards. They are very similar. Let's take a look at one such card. Allow students time to read the contents of the large card. Briefly go over each part answering any questions. Then divide into two teams (eight to ten per team is recommended). Hide the large card catalog card from view. Project the transparency which is not labeled. Give each team ten minutes to view the transparency and correctly identify as many parts as possible. Winners could be awarded laminated card catalog cards to use as bookmarks.

3. *Suggestion:* Though large labeled card catalog cards are available through most library supply companies, children definitely prefer ones made for their favorite books. Interest level will be higher if the cards are homemade. Use an opaque projector!

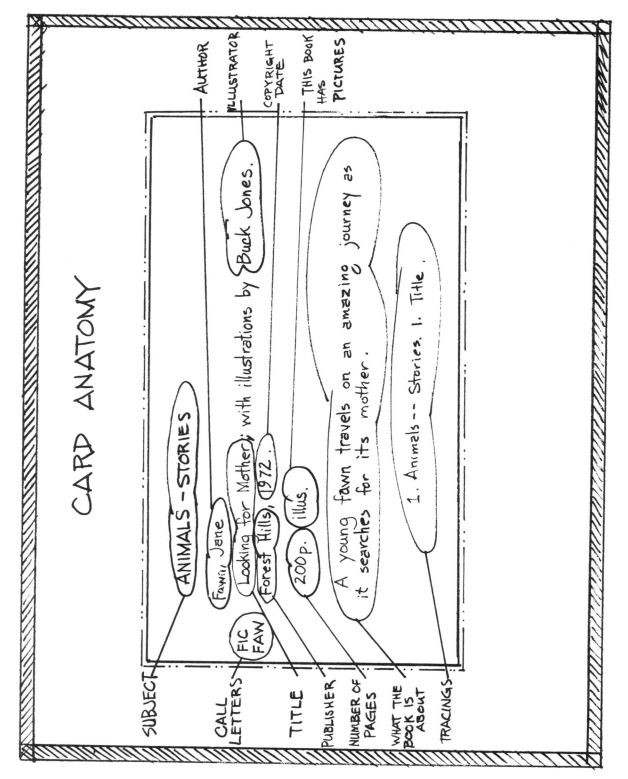

CARD ANATOMY

SUBJECT — ANIMALS – STORIES

CALL LETTERS — FIC FAW

Fawn, Jane

AUTHOR

TITLE — Looking for Mother; with illustrations by Buck Jones.

ILLUSTRATOR

PUBLISHER — Forest Hills, 1972.

COPYRIGHT DATE

NUMBER OF PAGES — 200p.

illus.

THIS BOOK HAS PICTURES

WHAT THE BOOK IS ABOUT — A young fawn travels on an amazing journey as it searches for its mother.

TRACINGS — 1. Animals -- Stories. 1. Title.

4-16 ONE EQUALS THREE (4-6)

Objective: After completing this activity the student should be able to recognize an author, subject, and title card.

Materials Needed:

- transparency of author card with overlays of subject card and title card
- enough extra card catalog cards for each child

Procedure:

1. Review concept that each media item has three cards in the card catalog: an author card, a subject card, and a title card. Using the transparencies, show the similarity between the three card catalog cards for a book. Point out that all cards are "author cards" to begin with and that additional information changes one to a title card and one to a subject card.

2. Let's continue. Explain that we are going to see how well everyone listened for details. Give each child a card catalog card explaining that *only* he/she should see it. When everyone has a card, ask students to determine which type of card they have...author, subject, or title. Ask those with author cards to meet in one area, those with subject cards, in another, and those with title cards to remain seated. Have them check each other for accuracy.

3. *Suggestion*: If group size permits, have each student softly say their author's last name and see if a matched trio can find each other (bearing all three cards for the same book).

4-17 NUMBER PULL-EEZE (4-6)

Objective: After completing this activity the student should be able to use the card catalog system.

Materials Needed:

- transparencies of author card, title card
- pencils
- copies of "Number Pull-Eeze" sheets

Procedure:

1. Remind students that an author card has the author's name at the top of the card, *last* name first. Also, review with them the rule that in the card catalog, title cards beginning with "A," "An," or "The" drop the first word and are alphabetized by the second word in the title. Here is the challenge.

2. Students are to receive a list of titles which include numbers in their titles. (Example: *The Eighteenth Emergency*). Students are to look up the books by either the author or the title card and find the missing number.

3. Numbers are then added together for a grand total. This is recorded in the space provided. When all have finished (or when time is up) the total is announced.

4. *Suggestions*:

   — Large teams may not be as effective in this activity as a few teams will dominate. Individuals or pairs are recommended.

   — Congestion around the card catalog may be alleviated if drawers in use are removed and taken to tables. *Note*: They *must* be carefully returned.

Name _____

Number Pull...eeze...

TOTAL _____

Directions: Here are some titles containing numbers. Use the card catalog to find the missing numbers. Then add them together and record your total.

1. A. A. Milne

   Now We Are _____

2. Eleanor Estes

   The _____ Dresses

3. Jules Verne

   Around the World in _____ Days

4. Betsy Byars

   The _____ Emergency

5. Theo LeSieg

   _____ Apples Up On Top

6. Meindert DeJong

   The House of _____ Fathers

7. Miska Miles

   Annie and the Old _____

8. Irene Hunt

   Across _____ Aprils

9. William Pene duBois

   _____ Balloons

10. Dorothy Spicer

    _____ Ghosts

11. Nonny Hogrogian

    _____ Fine Day

12. Judy Delton

    _____ Good Friends

13. Hans Christian Anderson

    _____ Tales

14. Aliki

    _____ Gold Pieces

15. Dr. Seuss

    _____ Fish, _____ Fish,

    Red Fish, Blue Fish

4-18 COPY CATS! (4-6)

Objective: After completing this activity the student should be able to find books using the card catalog system.

Materials Needed:

- copies of cat pattern
- books
- blank card catalog cards (to be used as clue cards)

- felt pens, markers—several colors

Procedure:

1. Prior to this activity: Books must be chosen. Following the examples shown here, clue cards should be written and inserted in the appropriate places in the card catalog. The cut-out cat patterns should be hidden in the back pages of the chosen books and books should be replaced on shelves.

2. Description of activity: Students should be reminded of the three main *types* of cards. Remember that there may be joint authors or two subject cards. Explain that this game should help them unveil *all* existing card catalogs for a particular book and then lead them to the actual book where a surprise is waiting for them in the back pages. Students are divided into small groups (six maximum) and group leaders receive the first clue card. When this leads the group correctly to the first card catalog card, their second clue card is *behind* that one. The search continues until all cards have been found and the book is discovered with the cat pattern.

3. Suggestions:

   — If students leave clue cards in their same place within the card catalog, groups can switch searches for a second round of fun. They need only replace the cats and properly shelve the books.

   — Noise level can be a problem unless students are cautioned in advance. Excitement rises as clue cards are discovered.

   — It is helpful to color code the clue cards (one group—red, next—blue, etc.).

Hand to group captain

1st Clue:

     Joanna Cole wrote this book about insects hiding.

●

Found behind author card: Cole, Joanna

2nd Clue:

     Good job! You found the author card. Do you see the other author's name? Can you find him?

●

Found behind joint author's card: Wexler, Jerome

3rd Clue:

     Not bad! Now you're ready for the title card. No problem, right?

●

Found behind the title card: *Find the hidden insect*

4th Clue:

O.K., I'm impressed!
I can tell you're "hot on the trail." Let's try a subject card. Look under INSECTS— HABITS AND BEHAVIOR !

●

Found behind the first subject card: INSECTS—HABITS AND BEHAVIOR

5th Clue:

Wow! That was hard, right!?! Now try a second subject card. Can you find it at the bottom of the card? Right! CAMOUFLAGE (Biology)!

●

Found behind the second subject card: CAMOUFLAGE (BIOLOGY)

6th Clue:

Yea! Super! Now for the most important part. Look in the left hand corner (top). Find the call numbers. Find that section on the shelves. Find the book... And a SURPRISE !

●

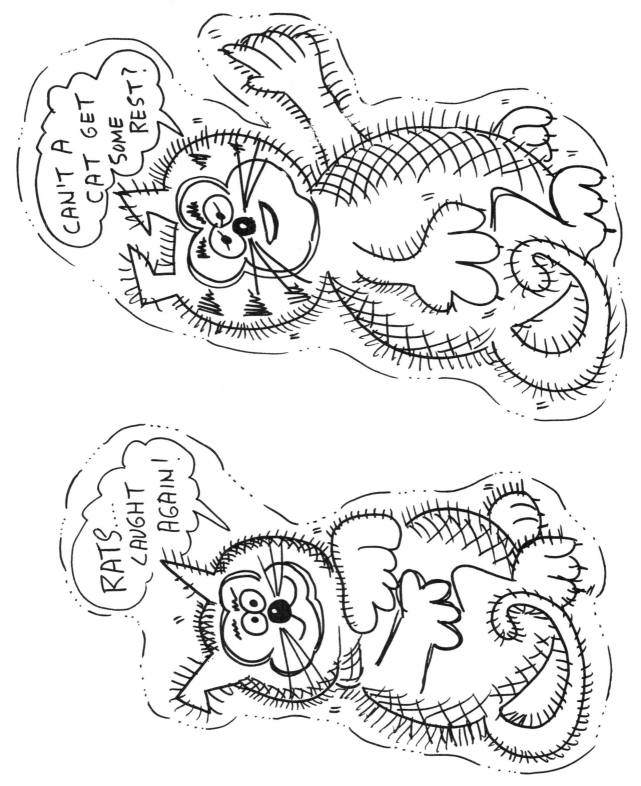

4-19 CREATE A CARD (4-6)

Objective: After completing this activity the student should be able to design his or her own card catalog card.

Materials Needed:

- copies of blank card catalog card   • pencils
  sheet

Procedure:

1. As a culmination to this unit on card catalog usage, encourage each child to fill in the blank sheet provided to make a card catalog card for the book he/she chooses (may be subject, author, or title card).
2. The student may refer to a card catalog for format.
3. Encourage child to complete at least:

   — Call numbers (letters)

   — Author

   — Title

   — Number of pages, illustrations

   — Publisher

   — Date of publication

   — Summary

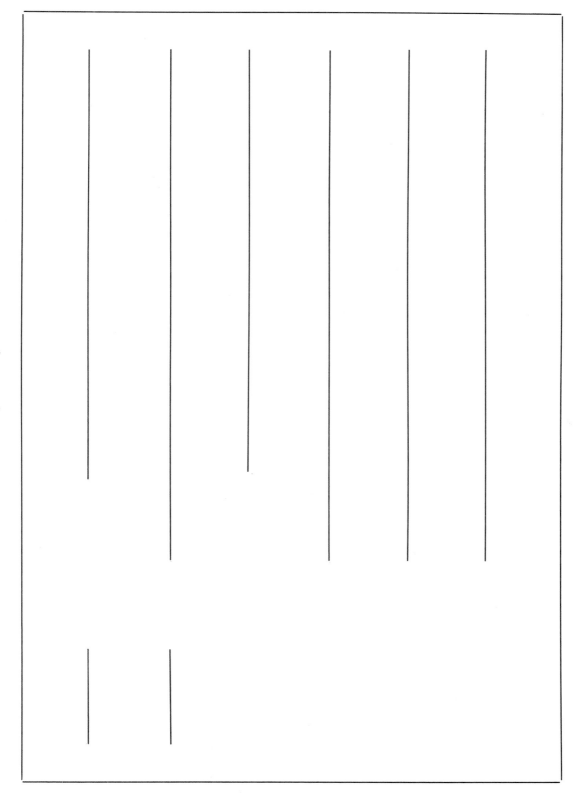

Dictionary Delight

Dictionary Delight (dik′-sha-ner′-ē di-l īt) has been specially prepared because so many of us have found the dictionary to be indispensible to writing and research. The following activities will enhance your students' dictionary skills in exciting and new ways.

4-20 THE "GUIDE"-ING LIGHT (4-6)

Objective: After completing this activity the student should be able to utilize guide words.

Materials Needed:

- transparency marker
- transparency of a dictionary page (preferably an intermediate dictionary in large print— *Webster's New Elementary Dictionary* works well)

- 10 to 12 dictionaries
- overhead projector

Procedure:

1. Show transparency and ask students if anyone can identify the "guide words." After correctly locating them, circle the "guide words" with a marker and discuss their functions. Emphasize the fact that they greatly increase speed in locating words.
2. Divide class into small groups. Give each group a dictionary. After students have familiarized themselves with the dictionaries, explain that you will have a relay to see which group can look up words the fastest. Caution must be given so students avoid yanking out the pages. Remind groups to use the "guide words" at the top of each page. Try several rounds orally. Provide

words and time the groups during the search. Now hand out a list of words (groups may use the same list, or may create different ones). After 10 to 15 minutes, see which group is in the lead.

3. *Suggestion*: Walk around during this exercise noticing which groups are using the guide words.

4-21 "GUIDE" TO MATH (4-6)

Objective: After completing this activity the student should be able to gain proficiency in using guide words.

Materials Needed:

- sheets for students to fill in
- pencils

- dictionaries for each child, if possible (dictionaries used must be the same as the one used to make the game)

Procedure:

1. Now that students know what guide words are and how to use them, this game should provide good practice. It requires an ability to add two-digit and three-digit numbers. A pair of guide words is given. When found in the dictionary the page number is recorded. Another pair of guide words should be given, found, and the page number recorded. Then the two page numbers are added and the total is used as a new page number whose guide words must be recorded.

2. Here is an example:

GUIDE WORDS:	PAGE NUMBERS:
Drill/Drown	158
plus	+ 239
Home/Honk	
Prettier/Primary	397

3. Suggestions: Obviously this must be designed:

— with your students' math abilities in mind

— for use with *your* dictionaries, but the examples shown in the following illustration should help get you started

Guide Words	Page Numbers
armadillo/arriving	27
beech/Belgian	+46
canter/capitalizing	73
actor/adjective	7
bound/brace	+59
bulkier/bur	66
garden/gaunt	208
duct/durable	+160
passable/pasturing	368
host/hovel	242
mob/mold	+322
univalve/unparalleled	564

4-22 TWO-CLUE TEASERS (4-6)

Objective: After completing this activity the student should be able to solve problems using guide words and page numbers.

Materials Needed:

- copies of "Two-Clue Teasers" sheet
- one dictionary for each child
- pencils

Procedure:

1. Explain to students that in each case, they must use the two clues (guide words plus another clue) given on the sheet to find the answer. Having students record the page number should prevent an inordinate amount of guessing.
2. Allow 10 to 15 minutes for completion. Take time to check together. Encourage those who finish early to design additional "teasers" for their classmates.

2 - Clue Teasers

Clues	Answers	Page Numbers
Example:		
a. palette/panic (guide words)		
b. cooked on a griddle (additional clue)	PANCAKE	363
1. a. fireplace/fizzling		
b. breathes with gills	_____	_____
2. a. diminish/direct		
b. means "terrible lizard"	_____	_____
3. a. loom/lounging		
b. noisy	_____	_____
4. a. ruthless/safe		
b. first day of the week	_____	_____
5. a. lithe/loaf		
b. South American cud-chewing animal	_____	_____
6. a. creel/crisp		
b. a manger for feeding animals	_____	_____

4-23 A NÜ LANG'-GWIJ (4-6)

Objective: After completing this activity the student should be able to use the pronunciation key in a dictionary.

Materials Needed:

- overhead projector
- transparency of a paragraph illustrating phonetic respelling
- one dictionary for each student

- copies of nursery rhymes for students to respell
- paper
- pencils

Procedure:

1. Hand each child a dictionary. Have each child locate the Pronunciation Key in the front. Discuss briefly any symbols that look very unusual (the schwa, "ə," for example). Then ask each child to write his/her own name phonetically using the symbols given in the key. Assist those who have difficulty.

2. Project the transparency of the phonetically respelled paragraph. (See the following illustration as an example.)

3. Allow students to take turns reading aloud, attempting to decipher the sentences.

This shood giv yoo səm prak'tis in re'ding re-speld wurdz. If we rot wurdz thə wa tha soun'ded, ow'r lang'gwij wood be məch sim'pler, bət we hav me'ne waz əv sa'ing thə sam groopz əv le'terz. Thatz wi we ned dik'shen-ar-ez too help əs owt. Tha tel əs hou too sa, or pro-nouns', wurdz.

---

4. Then pass out dittoed sheets with the rhymes for students to translate into phonetic symbols. They may use their dictionaries to look some words up. Here are three nursery rhymes to help you get started.

> Little Miss Muffet
> Sat on her tuffet
> Eating her curds and whey.
> Along came a spider
> And sat down beside her
> And frightened Miss Muffet
> away.

There was a little girl
Who had a little curl
Right in the middle of her
forehead.
And when she was good,
She was very, very good.
And when she was bad,
She was horrid.

Sing a song of sixpence
A pocketfull of rye
Four and twenty blackbirds
baked in a pie
When the pie was opened
the birds began to sing
Now wasn't that a silly thing
to set before the king?

5. *Suggestions*:

— If the students seem to have trouble, have them work in pairs.

— Insist on accuracy in copying symbols and using accents.

4-24 HELP THE TURKEY TROT (4-6)

Objective: After completing this activity the student should have reviewed guide words, respelling, and the parts of speech.

Materials Needed:

- copies of gameboard
- copies of word list
- one dictionary for each student
- pencils

Procedure:

1. This activity is designed to review and reinforce the various functions of the dictionary. Answers may be recorded in the spaces provided on the gameboard.

2. Before beginning, a brief recapitulation is in order to be sure there is no confusion on parts of speech, respelling, guide words, etc.

3. *Suggestion*: Change this game, using the same format, to adapt to various holidays or units of study.

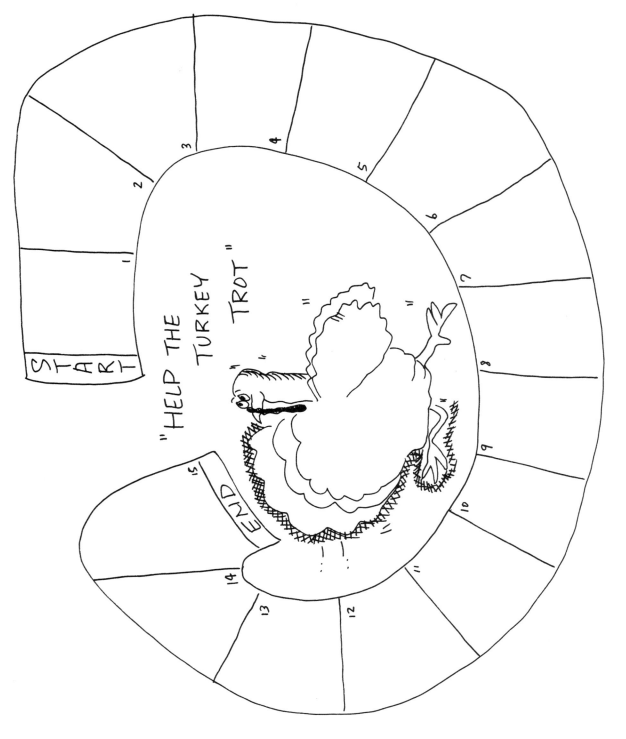

"HELP THE TURKEY TROT"

START

END

WORD LIST

1. respelling—turkey

2. guide words—pumpkin

3. part of speech—squash

4. definition—Thanksgiving

5. guide words—grateful

6. definition—Indian

7. part of speech—eat

8. respelling—gravy

9. guide words—pie

10. definition—corn

11. respelling—Pilgrim

12. guide words—harvest

13. definition—cornucopia

14. respelling—grapes

15. part of speech—thank

HELP THE TURKEY TROT!

4-25 IN OTHER WORDS (4-6)

Objective: After completing this activity the student should be able to use a thesaurus.

Materials Needed:

- dictionaries and several thesauri
- lists of proverbs
- pencils
- paper

Procedure:

1. Students should spend several minutes leafing through a thesaurus to become familiar with it. Students should be divided into small groups and given both a dictionary and a thesaurus. Each group should then be given a proverb and five to ten minutes to alter it by substituting different words or phrases, to say the same thing.

2. Groups may then swap papers and attempt to guess the original proverbs. For example:

     A coin of Great Britain freed from unnecessary waste is the same as shilling deserved as a result of labor or service. ("A penny saved is a penny earned.")
          or
     A deep, rounded container used for domestic purposes observed, as if by vigil, never has bubbles at the surface. ("A watched pot never boils.")

3. Other proverbs to use:

     — "A rolling stone gathers no moss."

     — "A stitch in time saves nine."

     — "Pretty is as pretty does."

     — "A bird in the hand is worth two in the bush."

     — "Ask me no questions; I'll tell you no lies."

     — "Early to bed, early to rise, makes a man healthy, wealthy, and wise."

4. *Suggestions*:

     — Each group could generate their own lists of proverbs after the first exchange.

     — Have some fun using higher level dictionaries—perhaps collegiate level.

TOPICS FOR FURTHER STUDY OF "RESEARCH ROUNDUP"

Presented here are more research possibilities. The topics require independent work. *Beware*: young researchers may end up detouring into uncharted waters of knowledge and study. Support these departures.

1. Compare and contrast biographies and autobiographies. Which do you prefer?

2. Design a file of provocative topics for class members to utilize. Students may want to develop their own files.

3. Design a board game which could be used to instruct your friends in the use of your school library. Incorporate the Dewey Decimal system into your design.

4. New facts are always appearing. Review the literature regarding how dinosaurs became extinct. Begin the review by examining literature copyrighted in the 1950s. Conclude with a review of material written in the 80s. Have the theories changed? What conclusions can you draw?

5. Astonish your friends. Develop a dictionary which includes faculty and student names with explanations.

6. Examine prefixes which are found in scientific terminology. Examples might include geo-, sub-, micro-, hydro-, and helio-. Investigate the origins of these prefixes.

BIBLIOGRAPHY FOR "RESEARCH ROUNDUP"

Dictionary Dig by Linda Schwartz (Santa Barbara, CA: The Learning Works, 1980).

Dictionary Dynamite: Basic Skills Activity Cards Using the Dictionary by Imogene Forte and Joy MacKenzie (Nashville, TN: Incentive Publications, 1979).

Dictionary Puzzlers by Jerry J. Mallett (West Nyack, NY: The Center for Applied Research in Education, 1982).

Hooked on Research! by Marguerite Lewis (West Nyack, NY: The Center for Applied Research in Education, 1984).

Library Skills Activities Kit by Jerry J. Mallett (West Nyack, NY: The Center for Applied Research in Education, 1981).

Using References by Sandra Brown and Sharon Levitt (Skillbooster Series) (Cleveland, OH: Modern Curriculum Press, 1976).

Section 5

LOGIC AND YOU

You will find that this chapter includes many activities which enhance thinking and reasoning skills. Students will be introduced to fallacies of reasoning, the concept of substantiation, thinking flow charts, and the logic and efficacy of rules. In the process of involving your class with these activities, you may discover your class debating the merits of a television commercial which used fallacious reasoning; or one which used an appeal to authority.

ACTIVITY TITLE AND GRADE LEVEL	SKILLS USED
Fallacies of Reasoning	
5-1 Appeal to Pity (4-6)	observing; criticizing; interpreting
5-2 Appeal to Force (4-6)	observing; criticizing; interpreting
5-3 Appeal to Authority (4-6)	observing; criticizing; interpreting
5-4 Appeal to Popularity (4-6)	observing; criticizing; interpreting
5-5 Appeal to Abuse (4-6)	observing; criticizing; interpreting
Flow Charts	
5-6 Cause—What Effect? (4-6)	problem solving; imagining

ACTIVITY TITLE AND GRADE LEVEL	SKILLS USED
5-7 Where's the Water? (4-6)	imagining
5-8 Flowing Ideas (4-6)	comparing; coding; classifying
5-9 Implications Flow Chart (4-6)	hypothesizing; criticizing; coding

Rules Around Us

5-10 Rules at School (4-6)	criticizing; interpreting
5-11 Rules at Home (4-6)	criticizing; interpreting
5-12 Rules in the Community (4-6)	criticizing; interpreting
5-13 Rule of Thumb (4-6)	criticizing; interpreting
5-14 Energy-Saving Device (4-6)	comparing; criticizing; interpreting; problem solving

Topics for Further Study

Bibliography

Fallacies of Reasoning

The following activities are designed to have students begin the process of thinking clearly. This will be achieved through the use of informal fallacies of reasoning. Among the fallacies to be considered are, "appeal to pity," "appeal to force," "appeal to authority," "appeal to popularity," and "appeal to being abusive."

5-1 APPEAL TO PITY(4-6)

Objective: After completing this activity the student should be able to identify the use of an appeal to pity.

Materials Needed:

- paper
- pencils
- room to act

Procedure:

1. What does the word "pity" mean? The fallacy of the appeal to pity occurs when someone uses "pity" to get an idea accepted. Here is an example.

   > Johnny had recently done several things that he knew might get him into trouble if his Mom found out. Well, his Mom found out! When Johnny's mother got ready to "ground" Johnny for his actions, Johnny stated, "Oh please don't ground me. I'm such a young child to be forced to stay at home for a week. Please don't do this!"

   > Notice that the use of "pity" is used by Johnny to try and get his mother not to punish him! Also note that Johnny was guilty of breaking some rules and did not attempt to justify why he acted as he did. Discuss Johnny's use of "pity."

2. See if students can develop an example of the "fallacy of the appeal to pity." Write an example. Be prepared to share with your classmates.

3. After students have written an example of this fallacy and shared it with their classmates, they should act out their fallacy. Other members of the class will study the acting to see where individuals used "pity" to make their point!

5-2 APPEAL TO FORCE (4-6)

Objective: After completing this activity the student should be able to identify an appeal to force.

Materials Needed:

- paper
- pencils
- room to act

Procedure:

1. What does the word "force" mean? Have you ever used force on someone? Sometimes older brothers and sisters use force on younger brothers and sisters! Hopefully, the force is not too severe!

   Sometimes the threat of force is used to get a point or idea accepted. This is called "the fallacy of the appeal to force." Following is an example of this fallacy.

   > Ann went up to her sister. She wanted her sister to play a special game. Ann's sister, Beth, did not want to play with Ann. Finally after begging Beth to play with her, Ann said to Beth, "If you do not play with me, I will break all your toys and pull your hair!"

   > Notice how Ann used force to get Beth to play with her. For a little sister, this could be an effective means of getting to play with her bigger sister. Discuss.

2. See if students can develop an example of the "fallacy of the appeal to force." Write an example. Be prepared to share your "fallacy" with your classmates.

3. After students have written an example of this fallacy and shared it with their classmates, they should act out their fallacy. Other members of the class will study the acting to see where "force" was used to make a point!

5-3 APPEAL TO AUTHORITY (4-6)

Objective: After completing this activity the student should be able to identify an appeal to authority.

Materials Needed:

- paper
- pencils
- room to act

Procedure:

1. What does the word "authority" mean? Who are some people you know that have some authority? The "fallacy of the appeal to authority" occurs when someone quotes or uses someone who may be an authority in one area, but may not be an authority in another. Following is an example.

> Sue was a great tennis player. She was considered the best in the world. On TV one night, Sue appeared in a commercial. In the commercial, she stated that GEE GEEs was the best possible cereal to eat for breakfast. Suddenly, Waddell jumped up and ran to his mother. He stated, "Mom, I just have to have GEE GEEs for breakfast every morning. Sue said it was the best breakfast and since Sue is the world's greatest tennis player, it must be the greatest!"
> Notice how authority was misused. Just because Sue is a great tennis player doesn't mean she knows anything about breakfast cereal. Advertisers often use people as authorities who may be an expert in one field but know nothing about another area. Discuss.

2. See if students can develop an example of the "fallacy of the appeal to authority." Write an example. Be prepared to share with classmates.

3. After students have written an example of this fallacy and shared with their classmates, they should act out their fallacy. Other members of the class will study the acting to see where "authority" was used to make a point.

5-4 APPEAL TO POPULARITY (4-6)

Objective: After completing this activity the student should be able to identify an appeal to popularity.

Materials Needed:

- paper
- pencils

- room to act

Procedure:

1. What does the word "popularity" mean? The "fallacy of the appeal to popularity" occurs when someone uses the idea of "popularity" to get an idea accepted. Here is an example.

> Jill wanted a new pair of jeans. She told her mother, "Mom, I have to have this type of jeans. All the girls are wearing them. They must be the best jeans one can buy."
> Just because all the girls are wearing a certain type of jeans does not make them the best one can buy. They may even be made of inferior quality cloth. However, Jill uses the popularity of the jeans as meaning they must be the best. What are some ways by which one could ascertain the quality of the jeans? Discuss.

2. See if students can develop an example of the "fallacy of the appeal to popularity." Write an example. Be prepared to share with your classmates.

3. After examples of this fallacy have been written and shared with classmates, act out the fallacy. Other members of the class should study the acting to see where "popularity" was used to make a point!

5-5 APPEAL TO ABUSE (4-6)

Objective: After completing this activity the student should be able to identify an appeal to abuse.

Materials Needed:

- paper
- pencil

- room to act

Procedure:

1. What does the word "abuse" mean? Have you ever heard someone being abusive toward someone else? Sometimes people abuse others physically. Other times they abuse someone verbally. The "fallacy of the appeal of being abusive" occurs when someone abuses someone verbally. Here is an example.

Mary was ten years old. Her brother Tim was fifteen years old. Tim and his friends were talking about great football teams. Mary said that the San Diego Chargers was a great football team. She started to give reasons for their greatness when Tim interrupted her and stated, "What do you know about football? You're just a girl."

Tim committed the "fallacy of being abusive" toward Mary. He did not argue with Mary about her reasons why San Diego was or was not a great football team. Instead, he attacked Mary personally. He was abusive toward her. Discuss.

2. See if students can develop an example of the "fallacy of the appeal to being abusive." Write the example and be prepared to share with classmates.

3. After students have written an example of this fallacy and shared with their classmates, act out the fallacy. Other members of the class should study the acting to see where "abuse" was used to make a point.

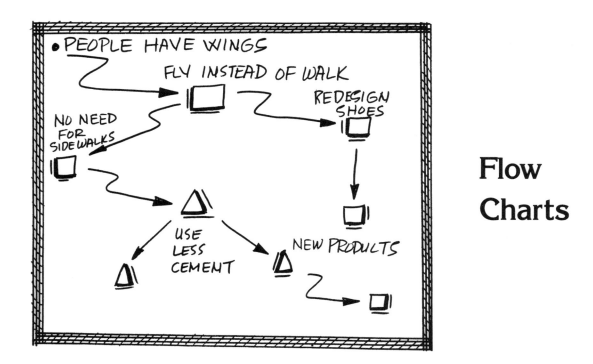

Flow Charts

The following ideas require that students diagram their ideas in a flow chart. Such activities can assist in building an improved understanding of causal relationships. Logical thinking is also enhanced.

5-6 CAUSE—WHAT EFFECT? (4-6)

Objective: After completing this activity the student should be able to describe the relationship between cause and effect.

Materials Needed:

- paper
- pencil
- chalkboard or chart paper

Procedure:

1. Begin by writing on the chalkboard <u>CAUSE</u> → <u>EFFECT</u>. Ask students to guess what the terms mean. Encourage them to give examples in their explanations. Now have students close their eyes and become very still for a moment.
2. In a very descriptive manner, have students imagine that they just received one million dollars. Instruct them to imagine what would be different about their lives.
3. Discuss this "cause → effect" orally as a group.

5-7 WHERE'S THE WATER? (4-6)

Objective: After completing this activity the student should be able to describe possible effects related to a dramatic cause.

Materials Needed:

- paper   • chalkboard
- pencil

Procedure:

1. Write on the chalkboard, while the students have their eyes closed, <u>(CAUSE)</u> <u>All of the oceans have dried up</u> → (EFFECT)?

2. Instruct students to open their eyes, read what is written on the chalkboard, and think silently for one minute. Now it is time for brainwriting. Each student should take five minutes to write down possible effects. When time is up, pass your written ideas to a neighbor. Take two minutes to survey the neighbor's list of ideas. Can you add to their ideas?

3. Students write their additional ideas on their neighbor's paper and return to the original author. Students circle their best two answers.

4. Combine the best ideas on the chalkboard.

5-8 FLOWING IDEAS (4-6)

Objective: After completing the activity the student should be able to develop a cause and effect flow chart.

Materials Needed:

- large sheets of paper   • chalkboard
- pencil

Procedure:

1. Review "cause → effect" examples from the past activity. Ask students to take the example of people flying and creatively illustrate the relationship between the cause and effect. Is this difficult?

2. Demonstrate using a "flow chart" to illustrate the cause → effect relationship.

3. Using a free-wheeling approach, students can brainstorm potential effects (any effect can come off of the cause or off of another effect).
   For example:

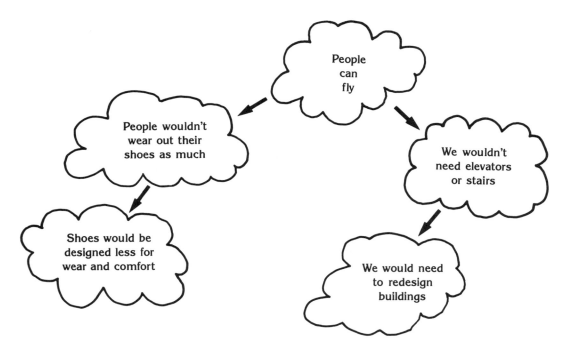

4. Pass out large sheets of paper. Have students draw a big circle at the top of their paper. Give students a cause from cause list (appendix) or have students generate their own idea for a main (beginning) cause. Instruct students to design a flow chart of effects, illustrating each effect with a connected circle.

5-9 IMPLICATIONS FLOW CHART (4-6)

Objective: After completing this activity the student should be able to develop an Implications Flow Chart.

Materials Needed:

- copies of "Implications Flow Chart"
- chalkboards
- pencils

Procedure:

1. Begin this activity by reviewing the previous free-association "cause →
effect" activity. Discuss the randomness of the associations. Point out the
no-limit approach to the generation of ideas. Students could have many
effects from one cause or many effects generated from other effects.

2. Pass out blank Implications Flow Charts to each student. Allow students time to decide what they will do with the charts. Ask them to brainstorm the limits of this style of chart. What would they do if they wanted to have two effects coming from the same cause? This format is designed to make the student isolate their ideas and generate a more focused effect. See the list of Flow Chart Ideas below for beginning causes.

3. After students complete the flow charts, encourage sharing of ideas.

Implications Flow Chart Ideas:

Imagine that:

— Your books could talk to you.

— Children had to hold jobs.

— Sweets were good for your health.

— Animals could talk and think as humans do.

— All telephones were like TVs and you could see the person with whom you are speaking.

— The government passed a law that all children under 21 would have to wear uniforms.

— Horses could fly.

— The sun didn't set one day.

— The earth stopped rotating on its axis.

— Our moon was destroyed.

— There was communication with life on Mars.

— Children didn't have to go to school.

— You were suddenly very rich.

— You were suddenly very poor.

— It rained jellybeans one day.

— Your climate completely changed.

Rules
Around Us

The following activities are designed to illustrate to students the function of rules within our homes, schools, and community. Students will find these activities intellectually challenging and highly motivating.

5-10 RULES AT SCHOOL (4-6)

Objective: After completing this activity the student should be able to describe the utility of rules at school.

Materials Needed:

- paper
- pencil
- coloring paper
- crayons

Procedure:

1. A good way to start an adventure with rules is to learn about the rules one follows at school. Perhaps a way to begin this lesson is as follows:

> "Did you children know that adults like me need to follow rules? I follow rules in school by letting the principal know who is here or who is absent from school. I also follow school rules by taking you to lunch at a certain time each day! Now that is a special rule and a fun one to follow!
> "Do you have some rules you follow at school? Let's talk about some of those rules. First of all imagine what would happen if a new student came into your classroom and did not follow any class rules. What might happen to the class? Would this be fair to the other students?"

2. Rules should be fair to everyone within the class. Can you think up some good rules to follow in class?

   WHAT ARE THREE RULES YOU FOLLOW IN YOUR CLASSROOM?

   •

   •

   •

   WHAT ARE THREE RULES YOU FOLLOW ON SCHOOL GROUNDS?

   •

   •

   •

3. Now make a poster showing one of the rules you follow while at school! What is special about following the rule on your poster?

4. Questions:

   • Why are rules at school important to follow?

   • What are some reasons for having rules at school?

   • Can you think of times when rules in school may not be fair?

   • Decide whether a school should have more or less rules.

5-11 RULES AT HOME (4-6)

Objective: After completing this activity the student should be able to describe how rules of the home help.

Materials Needed:

• paper   • coloring paper
• pencil   • crayons

Procedure:

1. Do you have rules you follow at home? Why are these rules important ones to follow around your house? Let's share some of the rules we follow at home.

   WHAT ARE THREE RULES YOU FOLLOW AT HOME?

   •

   •

   •

Are these good rules? What makes these rules good?

2. Questions:

- How do rules in your home make life better?

- When do you follow rules at home?

- Do you ever feel like breaking rules?

- What might happen if you break the rules at home?

- Why do you think the rules in your home are fair or unfair?

- What rules would you like to change in your home? Why?

3. Go home and talk to your family about rules at home. Find out what rules they had to follow when they were young.

5-12 RULES IN THE COMMUNITY (4-6)

Objective: After completing this activity the student should be able to describe the utility of rules in the community.

Materials Needed:

- paper
- pencil

- crayons
- poster paper

Procedure:

1. We have talked about rules we follow in our homes and school. Why are rules we follow in school and home important? We also follow rules in our community. People watch traffic lights for directions. Obeying the rules can assist a community in its efforts to be a safe and secure place to live.

You can think up other rules you follow in your community. Let's brainstorm two different lists:

Brainstorm a list of rules on how to treat people in our community.

Brainstorm a list of rules on how to treat things in our community.

When you have finished brainstorming, pick out a good rule to follow. Make a small poster showing someone in a community following this good rule.

2. Questions:

- Why do people follow rules in the community?

- What are some benefits of following rules in the community?

- Do you treat things in the community just like you treat people?

- What might happen if you broke the rules in your community?

- Can rules be unfair?

- What are some examples of unfair rules?

- What makes rules unfair?

5-13 RULE OF THUMB (4-6)

Objective: After completing this activity the student should be able to describe the utility of a rule of thumb.

Materials Needed:

- paper   - pencil

Procedure:

1. We have been learning about rules used in our lives. There are many rules we use and follow at home, school, and in our community.

People make rules. Why? People have reasons for making rules. What is meant by the word "reason"?

What are some good reasons why stealing is wrong? What is a good reason why you should treat people fairly? One should always try to give good reasons to explain why making a particular rule is important. We call this making a "rule of thumb!"

Today, we are going to learn about the importance of giving reasons for our rules.

   - Make a small list of rules.

   - Give reasons why these rules are good rules to follow.

Hint: A good rule to follow when making rules is to make a rule that everyone can understand!

2. Questions:

   - Why is it important for people to be able to understand the rules you make?

   - Why should the rules you make be fair?

   - Are rules easy to make?

   - Is it possible for someone's rule to be unfair?

   - What should you do if a rule is unfair?

5-14 ENERGY-SAVING DEVICE (4-6)

Objective: After completing this activity the student should be able to create a design for an energy-saving device.

Materials Needed:

- seven objects (toilet paper spool, paper clip, bobbie pin, rubber band, bottle cap, a construction paper circle—3″ diameter, and a triangle)

- 11″ × 18″ construction paper
- glue
- evaluation ballots
- copies of ribbon patterns

Procedure:

1. Inventing an energy-saving device is a challenging group effort in creative thinking and evaluation. In small groups, students will discuss their energy-saving device according to specific rules as they manipulate the seven objects on a large sheet of construction paper before gluing. Each group is responsible for a thoroughly written description of this invention which is attached to a device and evaluated by the teacher before presentations. Each group will introduce and defend their energy-saving device. Students will evaluate devices based on a set of criteria agreed upon by the class beforehand. Winning ribbons are attached to the best devices.

2. The teacher will evaluate the written description of the device and award a first place, second place, third place, and honorable mention award based on the most coherent written description.

3. After the presentations by each group, the students will vote on each project based on the pre-selected set of criteria agreed upon by the class. For example, if the class decided to have categories on:

     Strangest Device
     Most Practical Device
     Most Interesting Device

then the evaluation ballots would look like this:

BALLOT

Write the name of the group that had the:

① Strangest Device _____

② Most Practical Device _____

③ Most Interesting Device _____

4. The students would simply write a number next to the category. Each group is assigned a number to represent its entry. The ballots are collected and counted. Ribbons are awarded for first place, second place, third place, and honorable mention in each category. Mimeograph each ribbon with a different color to identify the places. Example:

> First Place: Blue
> Second Place: Red
> Third Place: White
> Honorable Mention: Green

Specific Rules:

1. All objects must be used.
2. Decide *which* energy-saving device will be used to conserve energy and *how* it will be used.
3. Each piece (component) must have a function.
4. Each piece must be labeled.
5. Give the device a unique title.

Suggested Criteria for Evaluation:

1. Coherent Written Description (Teacher Evaluation)
2. Most Practical Device
3. Most Appropriate Title
4. Most Creatively Written Title
5. Neatest

RESEARCH TOPICS FOR FURTHER STUDY OF "LOGIC AND YOU"

Presented here are a collection of topics for the curious mind. *Beware*: young researchers may end up detouring into uncharted waters of knowlege and inquiry. Celebrate these departures.

1. Review the writings and/or orations of a great philosopher. Design a dramatic production which recreates thoughts and/or oratory of the philosopher.

2. Compose stories that are illogical. Critique where the logic went astray. Analyze how the logic was assessed. Are there any attributes of a logical argument?

3. Investigate a current event. How might this event affect the future? Describe the alternative futures. Create a model of one of these alternative futures.

4. Compare and contrast a rule and a law. Also describe the differences between a law and a principle.

5. Conduct a debate of current events that has a protagonist and an antagonist. Discuss the results of the debate. Were any fallacies of reasoning used?

6. Apply logic to "if" statements like:

   - If I don't get caught who cares...?

   - If I just had my own stereo, I would be set...

   - If you would just get off my back, life would be much easier...

BIBLIOGRAPHY FOR "LOGIC AND YOU"

Ah-Hah! The Inquiry Process of Generating and Testing Knowledge (Resources for the Gifted, 4131 North 51st Place, Phoenix, AZ 85018).

Mind Benders—Deductive Thinking Skills Books (Resources for the Gifted, 4131 North 51st Place, Phoenix, AZ 85018).

Survival Skills (Resources for the Gifted, 4131 North 51st Place, Phoenix, AZ 85018).

Teacher's Gold Mine: An Everything-You-Ever Needed Treasury of Ideas for Creative Teaching by Dorothy Michener and Beverly Muschlitz (Nashville, TN: Incentive Publications, 1979).

The Unconventional Invention Book by Bob Standish (Carthage, IL: Good Apple, Inc., 1981).

Section 6

THE GLAD SCIENTIST

Included in this chapter are numerous activities which will delight students as well as pique their curiosities. From an encompassing journey through the senses to the development of energy-saving devices, the activities will help develop thinking skills and nurture the inquiring mind. Imagine dramatizing the demise of the "terrible lizards!"

ACTIVITY TITLE AND GRADE LEVEL	SKILLS USED
Dinosaurs, Dinosaurs!	
6-1 Dinosaur Book (K-3)	collecting and organizing data; summarizing
6-2 I've Got a Dinosaur on My Back (K-3)	classifying; comparing; looking for assumptions; problem solving
6-3 Dinosaur Jeopardy (K-3)	classifying; interpreting
6-4 Love Those Bones (K-3)	observing; collecting data; comparing
6-5 Gone Is Gone (4-6)	imagining; hypothesizing; looking for assumptions
6-6 They Are Known by Their Bones (4-6)	observing; classifying
The Human Machine	
6-7 The Human Body (K-3)	observing; interpreting; organizing data

ACTIVITY TITLE AND GRADE LEVEL	SKILLS USED
6-8 Body Awareness (K-3)	observing
6-9 Mixed-Up Body (K-3)	observing

Exploring Your Senses

6-10 La Premiere Cochon (The #1 Pig) (K-3)	observing; imagining
6-11 The Feel of Things (K-3)	observing; hypothesizing; collecting and organizing data
6-12 Henrietta and Taste (K-3)	observing; comparing
6-13 Henrietta and Smelling (K-3)	observing; intepreting
6-14 Hearing and Henrietta (K-3)	observing; interpreting
6-15 Seeing with Henrietta (K-3)	observing; interpreting

Ecology and Me

6-16 Weave a Web (K-3)	imagining; looking for assumptions; hypothesizing; interpreting
6-17 Ecology and Language Arts (K-3)	interpreting
6-18 A Pinch of This, A Dab of That (K-3)	imagining; interpreting

ACTIVITY TITLE AND GRADE LEVEL	SKILLS USED

The Wonder of Wildflowers

6-19	Wildflowers? (K-3)	collecting and organizing data
6-20	Data Sharing (K-3)	summarizing
6-21	Wildflowers and Mythology (K-3)	imagining; problem solving; organizing data
6-22	Walk On (K-3)	observing; collecting data
6-23	Compare and Contrast (K-3)	comparing
6-24	What's in a Name? (K-3)	hypothesizing; looking for assumptions

Topics for Further Study

Bibliography

Dinosaurs, Dinosaurs!

These six activities will introduce your students to the wonderful world of dinosaurs.

6-1 DINOSAUR BOOK (K-3)

Objective: After completing this activity the student should be able to identify various dinosaurs and dinosaur facts.

Materials Needed:

- copies of dinosaur sheets
- research books
- crayons

Procedure:

1. Begin by discussing information that would characterize one dinosaur from another (i.e., length, food it ate, how it got its name, how it protected itself, etc.). Through brainstorming, the students will produce a series of questions to answer about each dinosaur to be studied. Narrow the choices down to ten questions. Run off a ditto that contains these questions with blanks for the name of the dinosaur being researched and the answers that have been found.

2. Work on one dinosaur a day. The students research the given dinosaur, and try to answer each question independently or in small groups. Once they are done, the students meet to discuss the answers they have discovered. The students will find that their answers differ in some cases, and they will have to decide on the most appropriate answer. Once the answers have been agreed upon, the students will complete the ditto on that dinosaur.

3. Next, the students will color in the corresponding dinosaur ditto while portraying the dinosaur in its usual habitat. Once each dinosaur is researched the students will have an informative booklet for future reference.

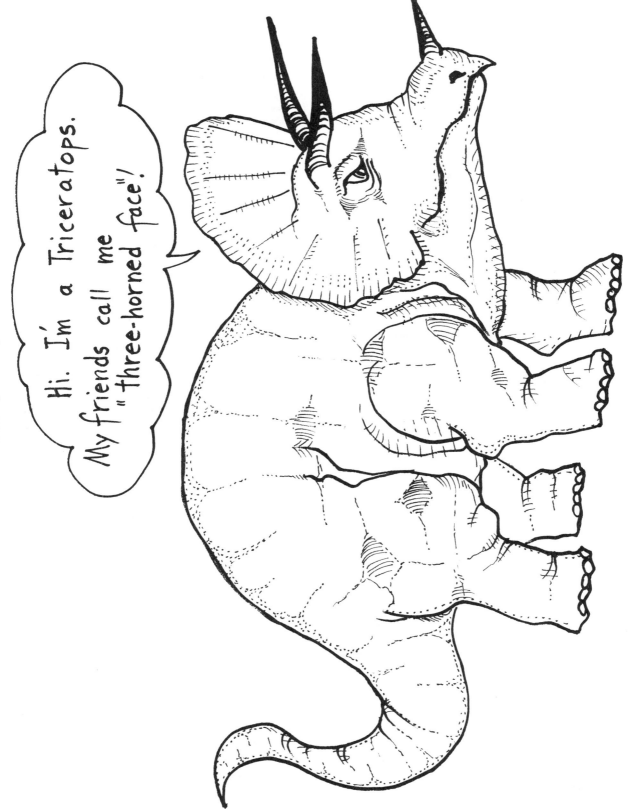

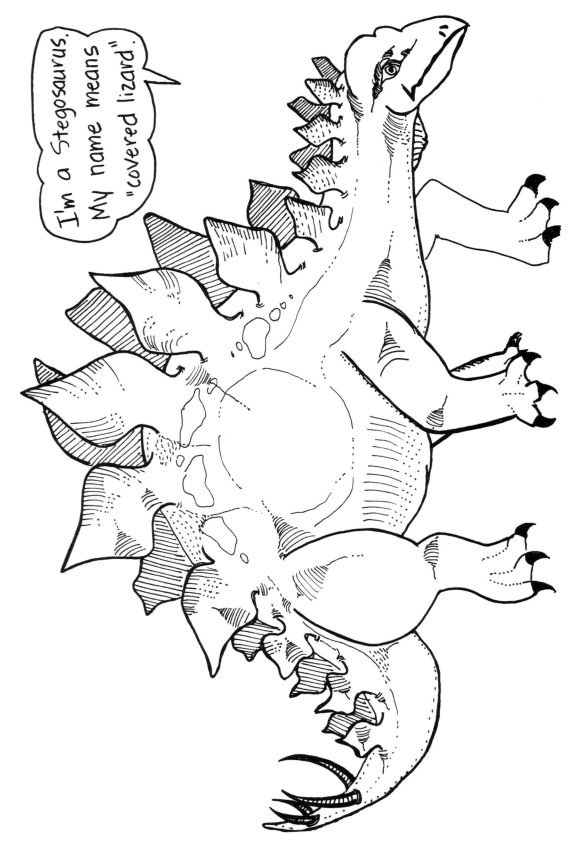

© 1987 by Artie Kamiya

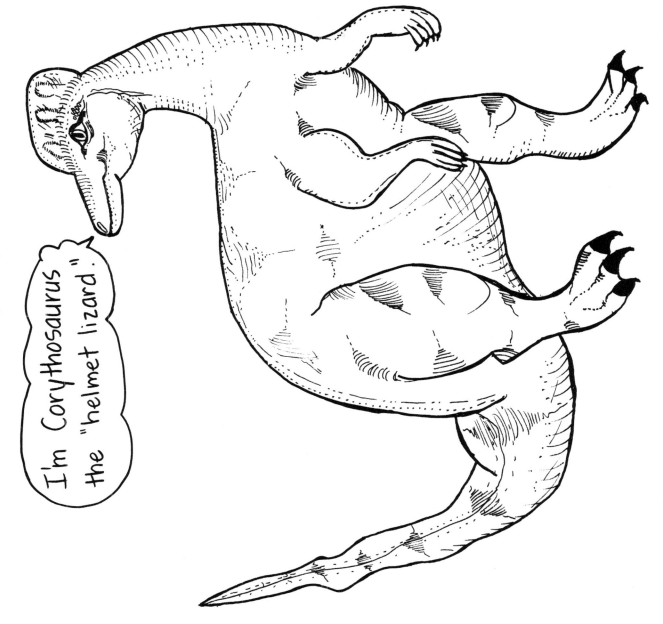

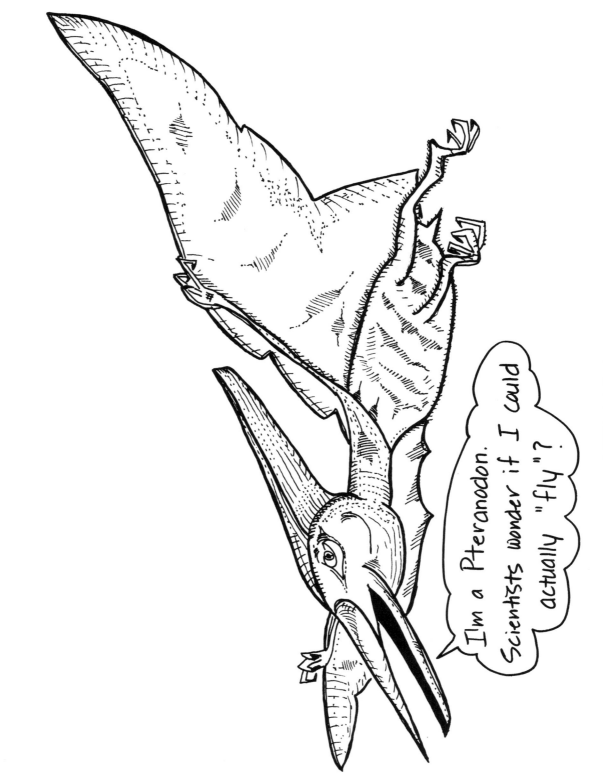

6-2 I'VE GOT A DINOSAUR ON MY BACK (K-3)

Objective: After completing this activity the student should be able to identify specific dinosaurs based upon facts related to them.

Materials Needed:

- dinosaur name tags
- tape

Procedure:

1. Each student has a name of a dinosaur taped on his/her back. The students mingle with each other while trying to find out the identity of their dinosaur.
2. The students ask questions about their dinosaurs that require a yes or no answer only.
3. After fifteen minutes the students guess which dinosaur they have on their back.

6-3 DINOSAUR JEOPARDY (K-3)

Objective: After completing this activity the student should be able to classify the dinosaurs using their known characteristics.

Materials Needed:

- dinosaur booklet
- chalkboard

Procedure:

1. Turn your chalkboard into a Jeopardy board using the ten research questions generated in the "Dinosaur Book" activity as categories for the game. Under each category, list six or more questions and value each question in ten-point increments.
2. Each team is awarded points for the correct response to each question. Once all the questions have been asked, total up the team's points and have them wager a portion of their total on the bonus question.
3. After the question has been answered, the team with the highest total is the winner. This is a good chance to check for retention of information from the students' research.

6-4 LOVE THOSE BONES (K-3)

Objective: After completing this activity the student should gain a better understanding of the similarities and differences between various dinosaur skeletons and their own skeleton.

Materials Needed:

- wooden Dinosaur Skeleton Kits (Animal Craft of Yonezawa Toys makes a series of these kits)
- tracing paper
- pencils

Procedure:

1. The students will construct the various skeletons without using the directions and check their skeleton with the kit's picture. Next, the students will identify the various types of bones (i.e., rib, pelvic, vertebrae, tail, etc.) of the skeletons.

2. The students will discuss the similarities and differences between the various skeletons and their own skeletons.

3. Next the students break up into groups to dissect the various skeletons making tracings of the types of bones and labeling the tracings. These will be compiled into a skeleton book with a section for each dinosaur.

6-5 GONE IS GONE (4-6)

Objective: After this activity, the student should be able to generate assumptions as to the possible demise of the dinosaurs.

Materials Needed:

- lined paper
- drawing paper
- pens and pencils
- crayons
- felt-tip markers
- resource books on dinosaurs

Procedure:

1. Read to the students several of the common theories concerning the demise of the "terrible lizards." Discuss how the world is thought to have looked when the dinosaurs lived here and how it looks now.

2. Encourage the students to use their imaginations to devise their own theories as to the extinction of these prehistoric animals. Provide lined paper and pens or pencils for this creative writing activity.

3. Students will make illustrations which will accompany the written reports.

   Theory Prompters:

   — Invasion by outer space creatures

   — Earth passing through a meteor shower

   — Giant volcanoes and earthquakes that changed the atmosphere

4. *Suggestions*:

— Short skits or plays can help dramatize the event.

— Relief maps may be designed to show the change in the earth's environment.

6-6 THEY ARE KNOWN BY THEIR BONES (4-6)

Objective: After completing this activity, the student should be able to have a better understanding of the major skeleton groups of the dinosaur body.

Materials Needed:

- white construction paper
- gray or blue construction paper
- scissors

- black felt-tip markers
- paste
- pencils

Procedure:

1. Have the students look through dinosaur books to find good illustrations that clearly show prehistoric animals. Each child will choose one illustration and use it as a guide. With a pencil, the basic skeletal structure will be drawn on white construction paper, carefully matching the general outline of the animal shown in the book. Make a list on the chalkboard of each dinosaur that will be used so that there will not be duplications.

2. Instruct the students to cut out the skeletons carefully. (It's a good idea to cut out the shapes in detail, but group the major parts. For example, group the ribs and spinal column. Individual bones can be very difficult to mount.) These skeletons will be pasted onto the colored construction paper. With the felt-tip marker, write the name of the dinosaur below the illustration.

3. *Suggestions*:

— Photocopy the illustration from the book and display next to the student's skeleton. Tack these to the bulletin board or on the walls of the classroom.

— Make a game by mixing up skeletons and book illustrations. The children will try to match each illustration with that animal's skeleton.

The Human Machine

An understanding of the parts of the body and their functions can be a very fascinating topic to the young inquisitive individual.

These activities will encourage your students to learn more about our amazing "Human Machine"!

6-7 THE HUMAN BODY (K-3)

Objective: After completing this activity the student should be able to have a greater understanding of the major systems and parts of the body.

Materials Needed:

- butcher paper
- pencil
- glue
- tape
- construction paper

- crayons
- scissors
- mirrors
- copies of body parts sheets

Procedure:

1. Begin this activity by tracing each child's body shape on the butcher paper. Have each student lie on the butcher paper and trace around the body with a pencil.
2. Cut out the body shapes and tape them to the wall. Have each student take a look in a mirror and draw his/her face on the appropriate place on the body shape.

3. Duplicate the body parts sheets found in this unit. Make a set of these sheets for every student.

4. In each of the following class sessions, study one of the body parts with the group. Explain the function of that body part to your students.

   Have each student color, cut, and glue the various body parts on their body shape. Continue until all of the body parts have been studied.

   Allow your students to take their body shape home at the end of this unit.

5. Additional activities: Use these ideas with this unit!

   Stomach: Use a blender to churn a complete lunch to show how food becomes liquified before the body can use it.

   Heart: Listen to the beats of the heart after various activities. Use a stethoscope after running, jumping, or resting quietly. What changes are there after exercise? Show the students a model of the heart. Obtain an animal heart from a butcher and let the students see it. Draw or tape a large diagram of the heart on the floor or on a sheet. Describe the function of the blood through the heart. Let the students pretend to be on a boat and row through the heart.

   Lungs: Have your students blow up balloons and let the air out to demonstrate inhaling and exhaling.

   Bones: Let your students feel their ribs, backbone, jaw, etc.

   Muscles: Let your students raise up on their tip toes. Go up and down several times. Feel the calf muscle. What is it doing?

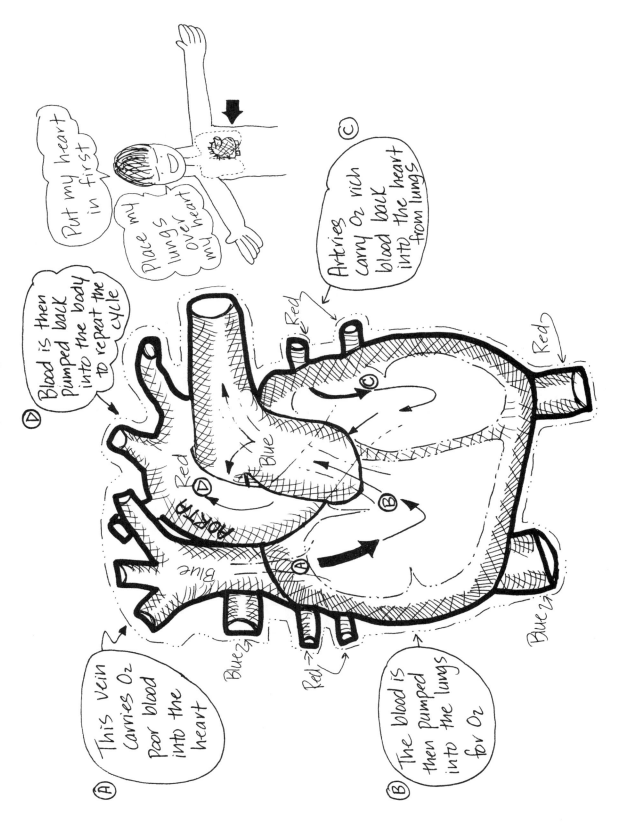

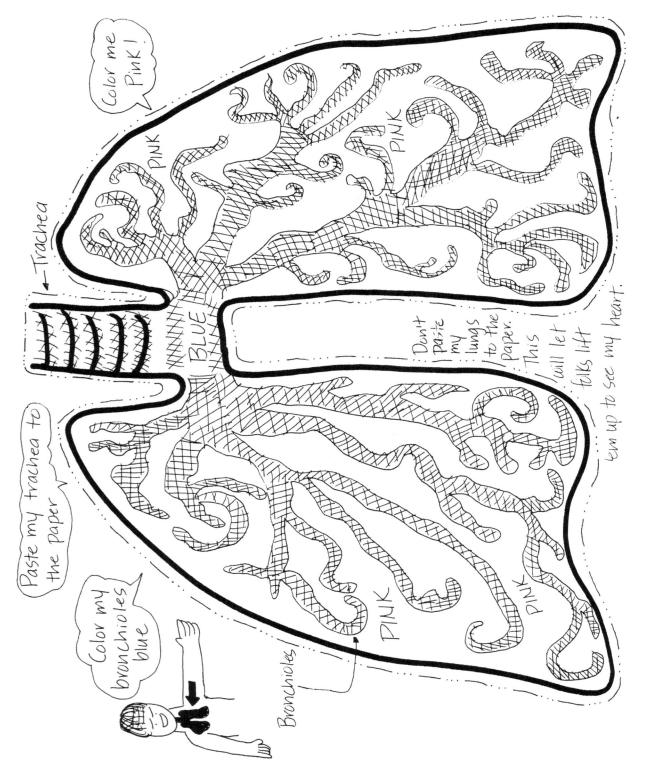

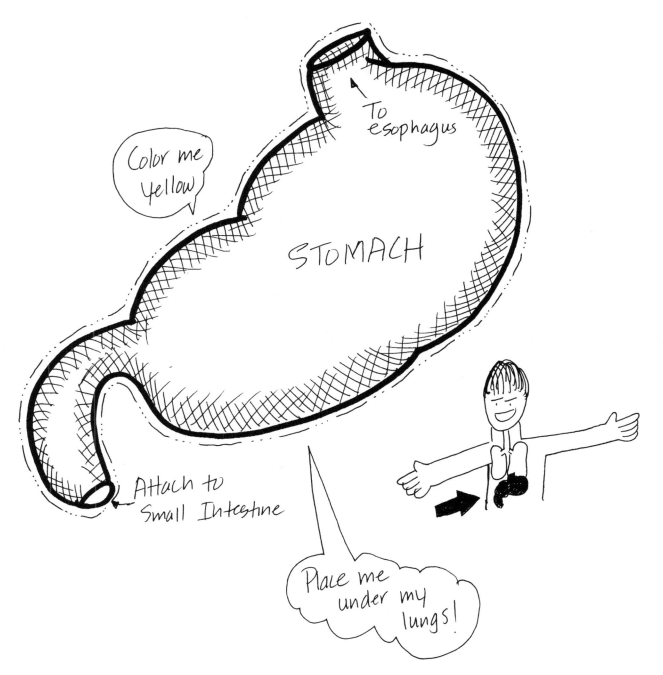

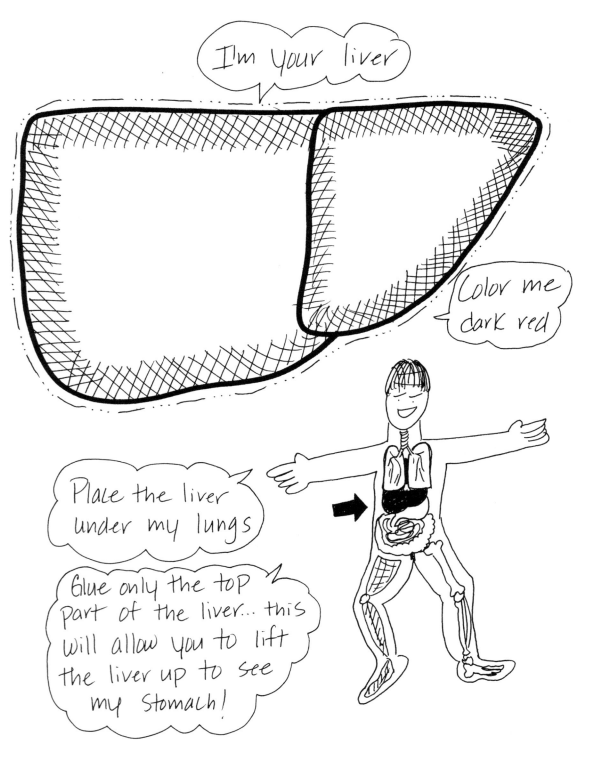

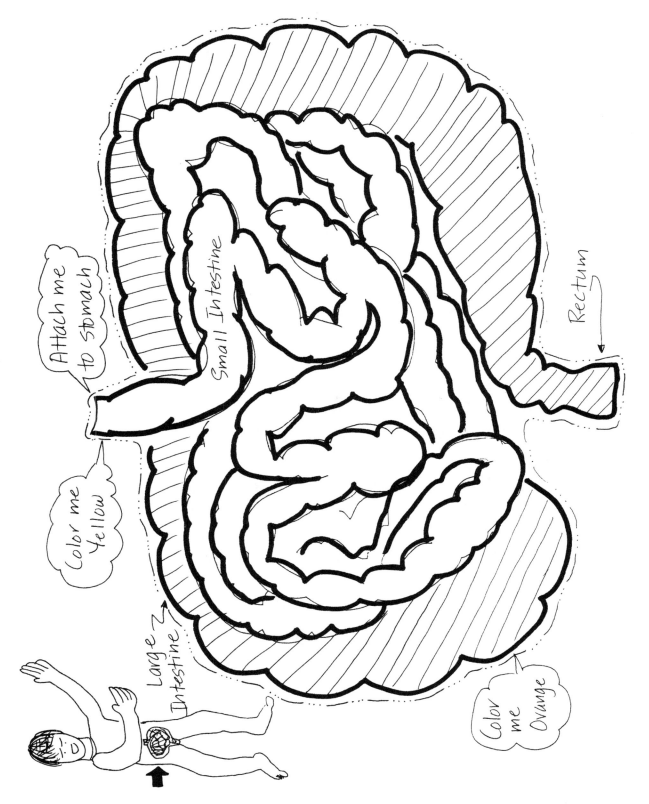

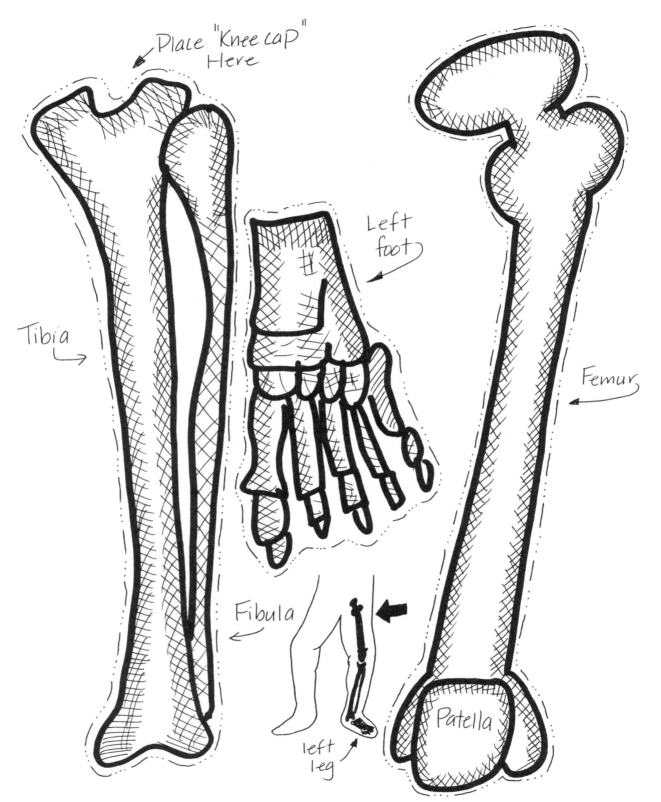

Place "Knee cap" Here

Tibia

Fibula

Left foot

left leg

Femur

Patella

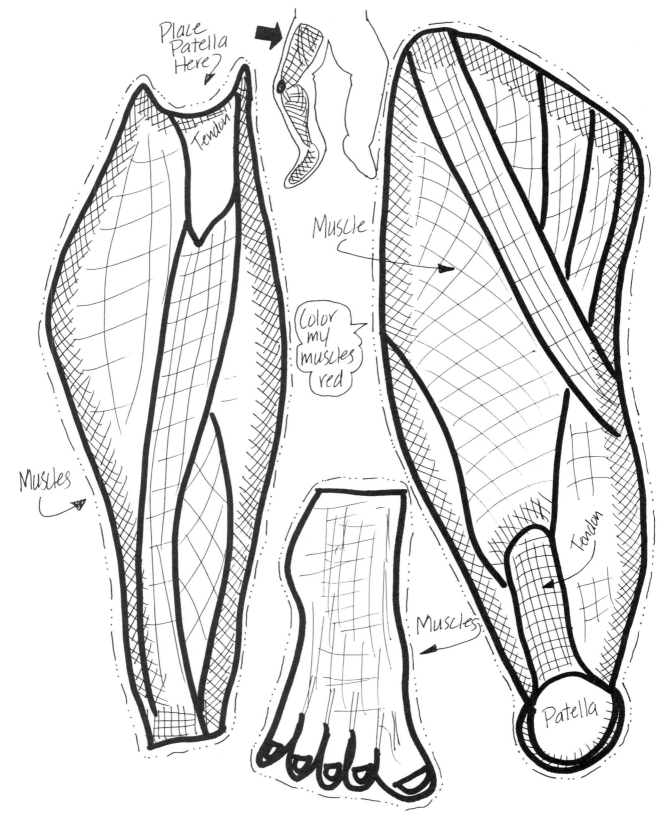

6-8 BODY AWARENESS (K-3)

Objective: After completing this activity, the student should be able to identify the bones of the body using their scientific names.

Materials Needed: none

Procedure:

1. Say: "Do you know what your body is? It's from your head (point to head) to your toes (touch toes)…It's all of you!"
2. Tell the students that you are going to play a game with them. They will touch the part of the body that you name. Work from top to bottom: head (cranium), eyes, nose, mouth, jaw (mandible), shoulder (clavicle), chest (sternum), legs, etc.
3. Repeat this activity and then call out the body parts in a random order.

6-9 MIXED-UP BODY (K-3)

Objective: After completing this activity the student should be able to recognize the different parts of the body.

Materials Needed: none

Procedure:

1. One person is selected to be the leader. She stands in the front of a group and begins the game by tapping her nose and saying, "Nose, nose, mouth." When she says "mouth," she taps some other body part, like the "ear." Players must touch what she says, not what she touches.
2. The leader will be trying to trick the other players. If a player makes a mistake, he/she is not out. Since this game is to help your students to learn where their body parts are, the students will remain in the game.
3. Change leaders often.

LA PREMIERE COCHON

Exploring Your Senses

Sensory experiences are important components of elementary science education programs. Our senses are essential to exploration and examination. The following unit provides a provocative sequential group of sensory activities which are guaranteed to excite your students.

6-10 LA PREMIERE COCHON ("THE #1 PIG" IN FRENCH) K-3

Objective: After completing this unit the student should be able to gain a better understanding of his/her five senses.

Materials Needed:

- bulletin board
- construction paper
- glue
- scissors
- yarn
- old gloves
- cassette recorder

Procedure:

1. This unit will be introduced to your students with the aid of "Henrietta the Pig." Your students will find out all about Henrietta and their five senses as they produce various group activities. The students first learn about Henrietta in this lesson.

2. But before your students can meet Henrietta, you'll have to make her! Here's how you do it:

   Find a bulletin board in your room and construct an oversized face of a pig, complete with arms and hands. Use yarn for hair, add some old beads, some old cloth for a blouse, and long white gloves for the hands. You'll find various pictures of Henrietta throughout this section. Use them as examples of what Henrietta could look like. Make your Henrietta as three-dimensional as possible.

3. Now, wouldn't you be interested in Henrietta if you walked into class and you saw her on your bulletin board! Now that you've gotten the students' attention, play them a special taped message (prepared by you in advance) from Henrietta.

   "Hello, Boys and Girls," Henrietta says in a rather obvious French accent. "My name is Henrietta. I'm constantly seeing, hearing, smelling, touching, and tasting things. Now, boys and girls...I want all of you to join me around my bulletin board...As I call you by name, I want you to quietly come up and sit down in front of me. Okay...let's see who's ready...(pause) Hmm...I think Fred is ready...Fred, please come here!" One by one each student in the class is called up by Henrietta. Once the whole group is gathered, Henrietta will discuss one of the following lessons on the five senses to them:

   1. The Feel of Things

   2. Henrietta and Taste

   3. Henrietta and Smelling

   4. Hearing and Henrietta

   5. Seeing with Henrietta

4. Feel free to pick and select each unit as you want to present it. You'll find a special picture of Henrietta with each of these units. The picture shows Henrietta using the sense that is being studied. You may want to enlarge and duplicate these pictures and give them to your students as each sense is studied.

5. Remember that Henrietta will interact with your students through you! Here are a few examples of how this may happen:

   — Writing a note to one of your students with a new dress stating that Henrietta "saw" the dress and liked it.

   — Leaving a bowl of snacks by the bulletin board for a "tasting party" after lunch.

— A short note to the student who happened to bring in flowers. "They sure smelled good," wrote Henrietta.

— At the completion of each of the taped lessons, Henrietta may give the students a special assignment to bring in a picture, object, etc., to reinforce the sense being discussed that day.

— Henrietta Awards: Interesting certificates could be made for successfully completing classwork during the unit. (See the sample shown on the following page.)

6-11 THE FEEL OF THINGS (K-3)

Objective: After completing this activity the student should be able to understand the various sensations that the sense of touch gives us.

THE FEEL OF THINGS

Materials Needed:

- pre-recorded message from Henrietta
- tape recorder
- duplicated picture of Henrietta feeling her puppy
- blindfolds

Procedure:

1. Turn on Henrietta's message. Remember to remind the students that Henrietta likes for them to gather around her. Encourage them to do so in an orderly way.

   "Well...hello...bon jour...boys and girls...Please gather around...."

   "Today we are going to talk about the sense of touch..." "If you were blind and deaf, you could still learn about the world around you. There are many small nerve endings at the end of your fingers and toes that help you identify objects."

   > (Pause here for discussion with children. You could ask the students what other body parts have the sense of touch...their arms, their face...)

   "The sense of touch helps you identify: hard/soft, wet/dry, cold/hot, curved/pointed, firm/mushy, and smooth/rough. The sense of touch is not only in your fingers, but on all of your skin. All the senses help protect your body from danger. If you had no senses, life could be quite dangerous."

   (Pause and discuss)

"I want all of you to bring something you can feel to class tomorrow to share with me. This is Henrietta signing off."

2. Discuss the assignment with the children. During their sharing time on the following day, blindfold the students. Ask your students to see if they can guess the textures and names of the objects they brought to school.

3. Give each student a picture of Henrietta petting her puppy. Let them color the picture or write a short list of the different textures one can feel. Have them give examples of the various textures too. Example:

Hard—Table	Curved—Wheel
Soft—Pillow	Pointed—Scissors
Wet—Water	Firm—Block
Dry—Paper	Mushy—Rotten apple
Cold—Ice	Smooth—Glass
Hot—Sun	Rough—Rocks

Ask them to think of objects that may have several textures. Example:

— Shoe—Hard, soft, curved, smooth

— Dish—Hard, smooth, curved, dry

— Brick—Pointed, rough, cold, firm, hard

6-12 HENRIETTA AND TASTE (K-3)

Objective: After completing this activity the student should be able to understand the four kinds of taste buds.

HENRIETTA'S TASTE TEST

Materials Needed:

- cassette recorder and pre-recorded message
- several hand mirrors
- various samples of tasty items

Procedure:

1. "If you look in a mirror at your tongue, do you see some tiny bumps? Those bumps are called taste buds, and today we are going to talk about them and the sense of taste. Can you see your taste buds?"

   (Pause and discuss. Pass around the mirrors
   so the children can see their taste buds)

   "Your tongue has over 9,000 taste buds. Small buds are in the front and large ones are in the back."

   (Pause for discussion)

   "There are only four kinds of taste buds: 1—sweet, 2—salt, 3—sour, and 4—bitter. The sweet taste buds are located along the front and a small part of the side of your tongue."

   (Pause and explore)

   "The taste buds that detect salty tastes are located at the front outside edge of the tongue."

   (Pause and explore)

   "The sour taste buds are along the side of the tongue."

   (Pause and explore)

   "The bitter taste buds are at the very back of the tongue."

   (Pause and explore)

   "The sense of taste and the sense of smell create flavor. When you have a cold and cannot smell, you cannot taste well."

   "Let's have a tasting party tomorrow! Would that be a good idea, Ms. Teacher?"

   You answer, "Why, yes, Henrietta. That's a great idea."

2. The next day have samples of different fruits, vegetables, and other items. Some should be sweet, salty, sour, and bitter. Use contrasting tastes—example: pickles and apples.

3. Explore with your students how the sense of taste and the sense of smell work together to create flavor. Have several students pinch their noses. Have them sample bits of onions and then pieces of apple. Could they tell what they were eating?

6-13 HENRIETTA AND SMELLING (K-3)

Objective: After completing this activity the student should be able to describe common smells and scents.

HENRIETTA AND SMELLING

Materials Needed:

- cassette recorder and pre-recorded message
- several hand mirrors

- various samples of tasty items

Procedure:

1. Turn on Henrietta's pre-recorded message.

   "Many animals such as dogs, pigs, deer, and bears have a better sense of smell than humans have. The nose that points back at us from the mirror is really an outside shell. It protects the delicate inner nose which has the important job of taking in air we breathe and smell."

   (Pause and discuss)

   "As you breathe, the air goes through two small holes called nostrils, over special sensitive cells in the inner lining of the nose, and into the lungs. Small hairs in the nose filter dirt. Can you describe some good and bad smells?"

   (Pause and discuss)

   "I would like to share this poem with you!

   What if your nose was all stopped up

   and smells could not get through?

   What if you couldn't smell apple pie?

Now just what would you do?

You couldn't smell a violet or cake

with nuts and spice.

You couldn't smell your favorite soap

or an orange that smells so nice.
                    (Pause and discuss)

"I'd like all of you to bring in things that smell. We'll smell them tomorrow."

2. Encourage your students to bring some interesting items to share in class tomorrow.

6-14 HEARING AND HENRIETTA (K-3)

Objective: After completing this activity the student should be able to identify several sounds and describe them.

HENRIETTA AND HEARING

Materials Needed:

• sound maker

Procedure:

1. Introduce hearing by using a "tuning fork," horn, whistle, etc.

"Your ears pick out differences of sound. Sounds surround us."

(Pause and listen to sounds in the room)

"I'd like everyone to go outside and listen for sounds. If you are quiet you will hear more sounds."

(Return and list sounds heard inside and outside)

"Our ears are used for hearing. The part of the ear you see is just a small portion of what you need to hear. It is called the outer ear. It catches the sound and lets it travel down a canal to the eardrum. The sound then goes to three tiny bones in the middle ear and on to the brain."

(Pause and discuss)

"Sounds can be high, low, soft, loud, happy, and even sad. People who work around loud noise protect their ears with earmuffs or earplugs. If you were an ear, when would you want to be protected?"

(Pause and discuss)

2. At the end of the activity, pass out a picture of Henrietta hearing someone speaking on the telephone. Let the students take this picture home, color it, and write down several sounds they often hear at home on the back of the sheet.

6-15 SEEING WITH HENRIETTA (K-3)

Objective: After completing this activity the student should be able to describe the different characteristics of eyes.

HENRIETTA AND SEEING

Materials Needed:

- pictures of eyes
- tape
- recorder

Procedure:

1. Turn on pre-recorded message.

   "Eyes capture the colors, patterns, shapes, shadows, beauty and ugliness, movement and stillness around us. When awake, our eyes rarely rest, so they get help from many parts around the eye. Can you guess which parts help?"

   (Pause and explore)

   "Bones surround the eyes and help protect them. Can you feel these bones? Eyelids also help. They serve as fast moving doors which help keep the eye moist. Eyelashes help by screening out dust particles. Even tears are important. Tears are made by two tear glands. Tears help clean your eye. How do you help to protect your neighbor's and your own eyes?"

   (Pause and discuss)

2. Direct the students to observe their neighbor's eyes. Discuss the various

   —shapes   —eyelashes

   —colors   —trace carefully the bones sur
                                               rounding the eye

3. Tell your students to close their eyes. Discuss blind people and how they frequently see through the eyes of a dog.

   — Explore the various shapes of eyes with your students. Pass out several pictures of people's faces. Does everyone have the same color and shape of eyes?

   — Give each student the picture of Henrietta looking at herself in the mirror. Have your students take this sheet home and try drawing a picture of themselves on the back of the sheet. Direct them to use a mirror and draw a picture of themselves.

   — When the pictures are returned, hang them up around the bulletin board picture of Henrietta.

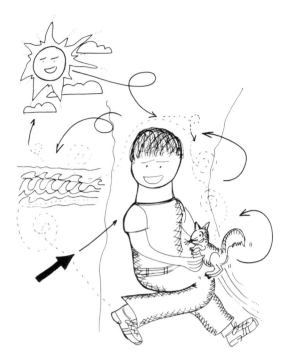

Ecology and Me

The primary objective of this unit on ecology is to enhance each child's awareness of the interrelatedness between him/herself and all other things. In this way, he/she will become more conscious of steps needed to sustain a more balanced way of life.

6-16 WEAVE A WEB (K-3)

Objective: After completing this activity the student should have a greater understanding of the different interactions between man, animals, and nature.

Materials Needed:

- ball of yarn

Procedure:

"Weave a Web" graphically reveals the interrelatedness of as many elements in the environment as the narrator wishes to include. Ideally, the ecology unit follows previous science units on all kinds of animals and plants.

1. With the children in a group, start an ecology story with an acorn. As the narrator mentions the acorn, the end of the yarn is given to the child designated "the acorn." The narrator then elicits answers from the group as to what an acorn needs to grow into an oak tree. As the appropriate responses are verbalized, various children are designated as air, sunlight, moisture, and soil and given a bit of yarn as the ball is unwound. The story

continues with the acorn growing into an oak tree that provides shade, homes for birds and squirrels, new trees from dropped acorns, and so on. All the while the ball of yarn is being unwound.

2. The children are beginning to become enmeshed in the web, and their ecological awareness is heightened.

3. Then the narrator interjects an ecological crisis. Factories could have polluted the air with some toxin, a forest fire broke out, etc. What happens to the elements of our web? With the help of the children, the narrator begins to backtrack while pointing out the damaging effects on the elements in this environment. The children see the tangled "mess" which could result.

6-17 ECOLOGY AND LANGUAGE ARTS (K-3)

Objective: After completing this activity the student should have an enhanced knowledge of ecology terms and their meanings.

Materials Needed:

- writing paper
- pencils
- dictionary

Procedure:

1. To strengthen language arts skills while focusing on particular science and/ or social studies units, incorporate various seat work assignments. For the ecology unit, have a challenge word vocabulary which includes some of the following words or phrases:

ecology	conservation
balance of nature	food chain
erosion	pollution
energy	environment
waste	recycle
ecosystem	overpopulation

2. The following activities incorporate the ecology vocabulary:

    — use the list as the week's spelling list

    — have the words arranged in alphabetical order and their dictionary definition written

    — using correct capitalization and punctuation, have the child write a sentence using each word correctly

— use the words to create word search pages, crossword puzzles, or cartoon strips

— create ecology word rebuses

6-18 A PINCH OF THIS, A DAB OF THAT (K-3)

Objective: After completing this activity the student should have a better understanding of ecological relationships.

Materials Needed:

- mixing bowls
- baking utensils
- ingredients for a real cake
- one-half of an old globe
- sample ingredients for an "ecology cake"

- stalks of grain
- honey
- toy model of a chicken
- toy model of a cow
- soil
- water
- balloon to symbolize air
- flowers

Procedure:

1. The objective of this activity is to demonstrate that all elements in the world have a special relationship to all others. They are blended in such a way as to benefit a product (much like a cake), or the environment in which we live. As ingredients are placed in appropriate bowls, the discussion of unnecessary ingredients for a cake parallels a discussion of unsuitable elements added to the environment. Discussion of the use of excessive amounts of some ingredients leads children into recognition of the harmful effects of overpopulation or too widely-used elements in our world.

2. As an optional special treat, the ecology cake could be placed in the sun to bake. Later it would be retrieved and substituted by a real cake for a surprise snack.

The Wonder
of Wildflowers

This unit incorporates many thought processes into a scientific study of wildflowers. The activities will enhance students' aesthetic appreciation and feeling for plant life in the environment.

6-19 WILDFLOWERS? (K-3)

Objective: After completing this activity the student should be able to have a better understanding about the needs of wildflowers.

Materials Needed:

- chart paper
- magic marker

Procedure:

1. Have the students discuss the following questions:

    — What is a wildflower?

    — Where do they grow?

    — Why do they need protection?

    — How do wildflowers get their names?

    — Are any wildflowers endangered?

2. Record student answers and ideas on chart paper. Mention that an important part of the scientist's job is knowing what questions to ask. Students may find that all the questions cannot be satisfactorily answered. Encourage research by teams of students. Each team is responsible for finding facts about a specific question. This would be a perfect time to have a wildlife educator or forest ranger visit your class.

6-20 DATA SHARING (K-3)

Objective: After completing this activity the student should have a greater awareness of the assigned topic.

Materials Needed: none

Procedure:

1. Research teams can now share the information they have discovered about wildflowers. Have each team select a spokesperson. The spokesperson will be responsible for sharing the team's collected data on the specific question they were assigned.
2. Discussion can follow the data sharing.

6-21 WILDFLOWERS AND MYTHOLOGY (K-3)

Objective: After completing this activity the student should be able to write a short myth about a name of a certain wildflower.

Materials Needed:

- book of Greek myths
- paper
- pencil
- scraps of construction paper
- scissors
- glue
- various outdoor nature objects

Procedure:

1. Begin by dipping into mythology. Read some examples of myths which evolved to explain some of nature's mysteries (for example, the Greek legend of Narcissus).
2. Have the students examine a variety of flowers, count the petals, note the petal shapes and the variety of pistils and stamen. Then have the students design a wildflower and give it a name. Their design can utilize scraps of construction paper and found objects from outdoors (sand, twigs, but no living plants). Once the flower design is completed, students can write a myth which describes how the wildflower got its name. Be sure the story contains:

   — a beginning (introduction)

   — middle (body)

   — ending (conclusion)

3. After each student has completed their story and illustration they may present it to the class. A booklet may be prepared that will contain all stories and illustrations. (What would be a good title for such a unique botany book?)

6-22 WALK ON (K-3)

Objective: After completing this activity the student should be able to identify and draw wildflowers as they exist in a natural setting.

Materials Needed:

- small booklets for note taking
- magnifying glasses
- colored pencils
- camera
- wildflower guides
- metric ruler

Procedure:

1. Take a field trip to a nearby forest or nature center. A couple of the spokespersons could be responsible for scheduling the field trip.
2. Students should draw discovered wildflowers first. Draw students' attention to minute details. Drawings should be colored.
3. Measurements can be taken and recorded alongside the illustrations.
4. Finally, students can use the wildflower guide to ascertain the wildflower's name. You may want to have students work in pairs as they collect data. Their research can be shared with team and class after you return to school.

6-23 COMPARE AND CONTRAST (K-3)

Objective: After completing this activity the student should be able to compare wildflowers with cultivated flowers.

Materials Needed:

- cultivated flowers in small pots

Procedure:

1. Ask students to examine a cultivated flower. Students should record all the similarities and differences between their cultivated flower and the wildflowers they saw.
2. Share results.

6-24 WHAT'S IN A NAME? (K-3)

Objective: After completing this activity the student will be able to better understand the name origin of selected wildflowers.

Materials Needed:

- *Wildflowers of America* by H. W.   • chart paper
  Pickett

Procedure:

1. List names of wildflowers on a chart. These may include:

   —Joe Rye Weed   —Jack in the Pulpit

   —Passion Flower   —Dutchman's Breeches

   —Cardinal Flower   —Dog Hobble

   —Trout Lily   —Iron Weed

   —Lady's Slipper   —Turtlehead

   —Crested Dwarf Iris   —Witch Hazel

2. Show the class pictures of some wildflowers. The student will choose one of the flowers above and dictate a story as the teacher writes. The story will contain the origin (refer to H. W. Pickett) of how the chosen flower got its name.

3. Each student will then have an opportunity to illustrate the story.

RESEARCH TOPICS FOR FURTHER STUDY OF "THE GLAD SCIENTIST"

Presented here are further topics for the budding scientist. *Beware:* young motivated scientists may end up detouring into uncharted waters of discovery. Encourage these departures.

1. Investigate insects and animals that have the ability to move at a high rate of speed on land. Compare their anatomical structures and angles of appendages.

2. Using various shaped cymbals and/or pieces of metal, discover the relationship of sound produced to size and shape of the instruments.

3. Descarte was one of the first to recognize the law of refraction. Investigate refraction and reflection principles. Demonstrate in a creative manner your findings. Diamonds are cut to maximize the reflection of light. Discover what angles are more reflective.

4. Research the transition between "flat" style paintings and when artists began to represent the world in three dimensions. Identify the beginning of the belief in the world as a sphere as well as early geometric principles. Can parallels be drawn between these major transitions? If so, evaluate.

5. Fish use fins for thrust movement. Investigate how people have developed thrust for transportation (airplanes, motor boats, etc.).

6. Hold your finger at arm's length. Look at it with each individual eye and notice the jump. This is called a parallactic shift. Research the term "parallax" and its applications to astronomy.

7. Identify reflective, rotational, and transitional symmetry in nature. Discover these same principles in architecture. Create models incorporating these forms of symmetry.

BIBLIOGRAPHY FOR "THE GLAD SCIENTIST"

Dictionary of Dinosaurs by Joseph Rosenbloom (New York: Messner, 1980).

Dinosaur Time by Peggy Parrish (New York: Harper and Row, 1974).

Field Guide to North American Wildflowers by The Audubon Society (New York: Alfred Knopf, 1979).

The Incredible Body Machine by Paula S. Brown (New York: Random House/CTW, 1981).

National Geographic World, National Geographic Society, 17th and M Streets, N.W., Washington, D.C. 20036. This is a great science and nature magazine for grades 3–5.

What Really Happened to the Dinosaurs? by Daniel Cohen (New York: Dutton, 1977).

Your Big Backyard, National Wildlife Federation, 1412 Sixteenth Street, N.W., Washington, D.C. 20036. This is an excellent nature magazine for children in grades K–1.

Section 7

VIEWPOINTS

The units of study in this chapter provide an extraordinary introduction to geography. Students will become geographers and once knowledgeable, will apply their skills to creative geography problems. Imagine your students specializing in one of the following: demography, climatology, oceanography, as they work to construct a diorama of the unique Planet X.

ACTIVITY TITLE AND GRADE LEVEL	SKILLS USED
Becoming Geographers	
7-1 Hocus, Pocus, Focus (4-6)	observing; collecting and organizing data
7-2 Touch Mapping (4-6)	observing; collecting and organizing data; interpreting
7-3 Visions (4-6)	collecting and organizing data; problem solving
7-4 Treasure Hunt (4-6)	interpreting; problem solving
Rearranging Our World	
7-5 Cityscape (K-3)	collecting and organizing data; imagining; interpreting
7-6 All About School (4-6)	observing; collecting and storing data; interpreting; problem solving

ACTIVITY TITLE AND GRADE LEVEL	SKILLS USED
7-7 Creator (4-6)	collecting and organizing data; hypothesizing; interpreting; problem solving
7-8 Things Would Be Different If??? (4-6)	collecting and organizing data; imagining; interpreting
7-9 Going Back in Time (4-6)	imagining; interpreting

Using Geography

7-10 Name That Continent (K-3)	problem solving
7-11 Geographical Bingo (4-6)	collecting and organizing data; interpreting
7-12 Map Fluency (4-6)	organizing data; classifying
7-13 This Is the Land that "Jack" Built (4-6)	organizing data; classifying

Applied Geography

7-14 Planet X (4-6)	imagining; coding; problem solving
7-15 The Great (Fill in Your State's Nickname) Race! (4-6)	problem solving; organizing data
7-16 The ABCs of World Travel (4-6)	collecting and organizing data; problem solving

Topics for Further Study

Bibliography

Becoming Geographers

"Geography" comes from the Greek word "geographia" which means "earth description." The following activities will help your student to become acquainted in a personal way with the concepts of geography.

7-1 HOCUS, POCUS, FOCUS (4-6)

Objective: After completing this activity the student should be able to use terms of geographic inquiry.

Materials Needed:

- paper towel tubes
- paper
- pencils
- copies of "Areas of Geographic Inquiry" sheet

Procedure:

1. The students are instructed as to the four areas of geographic inquiry. These are:

   — the location of places and people

   — how various parts of the "world" are the same/different

   — the development of features of the earth

   — the space relationships of areas to each other

2. The teacher should first divide the classroom into *quadrants* using masking tape on the floor or physical barriers such as desks. Divided into small groups, the students will use their paper towel tubes to "focus" on their assigned section of the room. Students may take turns writing as a fellow explorer describes the features of the room in geographic terms. (See the inquiry sheet.)

3. Students may practice and extend this activity to the school grounds, home, and neighborhood.

HOCUS, POCUS, FOCUS

Areas of Geographic Inquiry

EARTH LOCATION   (Quadrant 1)

Room features (walls, bookshelves, door, etc.) Give advantages and disadvantages of features.

EARTH DESCRIPTION   (Quadrant 2)

Describe how the space/surroundings influence what happens there; (the location of the teacher's desk influences location of student desks, traffic patterns, etc.).

EARTH CHANGES   (Quadrant 3)

Investigate any changes that may have occurred or may occur (examples: evidence that bookshelves have been moved, heating or cooling system changes, placement of learning areas, etc.).

EARTH SPACE RELATIONS   (Quadrant 4)

Describe how the earth space has been changed by people (examples: does building location influence what goes on there? How does the classroom location and activities impact neighboring classes?

7-2 TOUCH MAPPING (4-6)

Objective: After completing this activity the student should be able to describe a location through design of a map.

Materials Needed:

- large sheets of posterboard   • blindfold
- pencils/crayons

Procedure:

1. Students should remain in room quadrant groups as described in previous activity ("Hocus, Pocus, Focus"). One team member at a time should be blindfolded and placed in the *center* of the four quadrants. One team member reads the following directions and questions:

   Move _____ steps to the North (forward). What do you feel located there?

   Move _____ steps to the East (right). What do you feel located there?

   Move _____ steps to the South (backward). What do you feel located there?

   Move _____ steps to the West (left). What do you feel located there?

   Another team member is designated as the "guide" who is familiar with this "world's" boundaries. Another team member acts as the group recorder.

2. A strict three-minute time limit is observed for this activity. The blindfolded student is to be guided into an area and allowed to identify the surroundings through touch (a feeling map) for his/her teammates. If time allows, several members may exchange roles and compare their maps.

3. Using the information collected from the geographical inquiry (feeling map) students will transfer these descriptions to posterboard, drawing a physical map of their room quadrant. The instructor may provide a map scale so that the finished maps may be placed together to form a large, complete map of the room. This map may then be used to query the ways that the study of geography is useful.

4. What might happen if some of the physical features were changed? Suppose a valuable mineral were found in the north. What might happen to the surrounding physical features? What might happen if the teacher decided to locate his/her desk in the center of your quadrant?

5. On paper, with the blindfold on, draw what your earth location may look like.

7-3 VISIONS (4-6)

Objective: After completing this project the student should be able to use basic terms of geographic inquiry.

Materials Needed:

- several large wall-size general reference maps (state, United States, continents, world)

Procedure:

1. Familiarize the student with the map displayed by discussing the map using the four areas of geographical inquiry. (Refer back to the "Hocus, Pocus, Focus" inquiry sheet.) Describe an area by stating "These clues are related to…(earth location, description, changes, space relations). I am having a vision of a place where…" Provide a clue as to the area you are envisioning on the map provided. Continue to give clues until the students correctly identify the location that you are describing.
2. Begin this activity by using very broad terms and gradually give clues that would help to pinpoint the location. Students may be given a map and can design a "vision" to present to the class using specific geographical inquiry.

7-4 TREASURE HUNT (4-6)

Objective: After completing this activity the student should be able to use basic map-reading skills.

Materials Needed:

- maps (see the sample given)
- posterboard
- treasures such as pencils, erasers, and stickers

Procedure:

1. Divide the students into small groups. Each group should be given a copy of the treasure map.
2. Using the map scale, map key, and directions, they must locate the treasure. This can be a "paper and pencil" hunt or an "outside" hunt as shown in this illustration:

Directions:

1. Travel north of school entrance 20 miles

2. Then proceed 24 miles northeast

3. Continue 40 miles southeast

4. Now move 20 miles south—mark the treasure.

  1 step = 1 mile

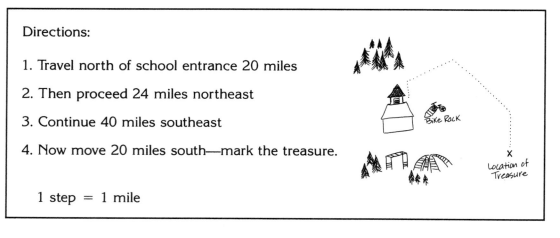

3. Suggestions: This activity may be used to review longitude and latitude. Provide the students with a map showing longitude and latitude as well as the longitude and latitude of the location of the treasure. Give a time limit to locate the treasure and turn the review into an exciting race. Include a teacher-made compass.

Rearranging Our World

"Rearranging Our World" is an extension of basic social studies concepts. A foundation of facts in geography and history is essential to the effectiveness of the following activities. The concepts which are introduced can be adapted to any locale and to a variety of age levels.

7-5 CITYSCAPE (K-3)

Objective: After completing this activity the student should be able to identify two consequences of a geographical change to their community.

Materials Needed:

- paper
- markers
- pencils

Procedure:

1. Begin by dividing students into small groups, four or five to a group. Have small groups brainstorm general natural resources and geography features of their local town or city. Small groups should share their lists with the class.

2. Instruct students that they have been given one wish: to change a feature of their local town or city. They may, for example, change its physical location, add a new natural resource like oil, or change the average amount of rainfall there. As a group, the students will discuss their choices and compile a list of changes that will occur as a result of their decisions.

3. Encourage students to predict all of the implications and consequences of making one change. Groups will share their change and its consequences with the rest of the class.

7-6 ALL ABOUT SCHOOL (4-6)

Objective: After completing this activity the student should be able to relate physical observations and geographic characteristics of their school setting to the design of an alternative school along with a written rationale.

Materials Needed:

- paper
- markers
- pencils

- assorted materials for building models

Procedure:

1. Explain to students that this activity will center on their school environment. Begin with an observational walk around the school grounds. Have students compile a list of all physical observations of the school grounds.

2. Ask students to include geographic characteristics of the setting. Once students return to the classroom, instruct them to circle their three most impressive or important observations and share with the rest of the class. Note with students general temperatures, rainfall, altitude, and vegetation in the area.

3. Explain to students that you are going to allow them to run with their imaginations and create a new physical setting for the school. They may include anything they think would enhance their education. Remind students that each change must take into account the safety of the entire school. Have students present their new settings in project form (i.e., drawing, model, etc.).

4. As a summary and integration of the concepts, have students write their rationales for the changes. These "position papers" should include how the design would better their education and how the design would impact the entire school.

7-7 CREATOR (4-6)

Objective: After completing this activity the student should be able to identify major geographical attributes of their state and predict historical outcomes due to student-initiated changes in their state's geography.

Materials Needed:

- maps of state
- drawing paper

- markers
- construction paper

Procedure:

1. Begin this activity with a discussion of all geographical facts of the student's state. Have students use maps for this review. Identify specific points of interest (i.e., large bodies of water, mountains, rivers).

2. Have students pretend they are reforming their state. Students are required to include all of the main geographical features identified in the earlier discussion. Explain to students that they have complete freedom to move these elements and can reshape the outside border of the state. Instruct students to think through their decisions. Using colored construction paper, markers, and drawing paper, have students present their new state in map form.

3. Finally, have students reflect on the history of the state. For example, early settlers were heavily influenced by mountains and rocky coastlines. Instruct students to apply historical factors to their newly formed state. Identify possible changes in history that would result from their design. For example, in North Carolina the mountains slowed down settlements to the west. If the mountains had run east-west, the settlers would have moved further west in less time. Share ideas with the class.

7-8 THINGS WOULD BE DIFFERENT IF??? (4-6)

Objective: After completing this activity the student should be able to describe at least three major events which shaped U.S. history.

Materials Needed:

- large chart paper
- markers

Procedure:

1. Begin class with a review of major factors shaping U.S. history. Record this list on the chart paper. Lists might include:
   — the Revolutionary War
   — the signing of the Declaration of Independence
   — trade
   — the Emancipation Proclamation
   — the Civil War
   — the Bill of Rights
   — the Depression

— the Women's Suffrage Movement

— World Wars I and II

— Computers

2. From the list generated, have the class identify the most significant factors. Create a time line representing these significant events.

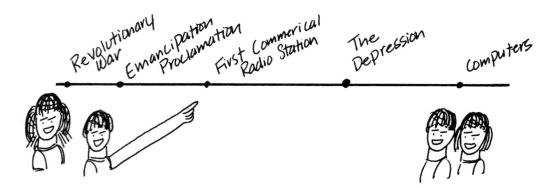

3. Explain to the class that they are going to isolate one of these factors and think silently for two minutes of all the things that would be different if this event had not occurred. Have students share their thoughts.

7-9 GOING BACK IN TIME (4-6)

Objective: After completing this activity the student should be able to take the perspective of an important historical figure.

Materials Needed:

• paper   • pencil

Procedure:

1. Ask students, "What makes someone in history famous?" Discuss the concept of being famous.

2. Have the students generate a list of famous people in history. Ask students to then write a short descriptive phrase which describes that individual. As a class, share the phrases and discuss commonalities.

3. Each student should then choose a historical figure to independently research.

4. On completion of this study, have students choose one of the following extension activities:

— Create a monologue with your historical figure as if you have just run into him/her on the street.

— Create an interview with your historical figure imagining that you are living during his/her time.

— Write a letter to your hero with the perspective that you are a member of his/her family.

— Write a narration about their life from the point of view of one of their pets.

— Create a monologue between your historical figure and another significant person of their time period.

Using Geography

This unit will assist students in learning basic concepts important to a thorough understanding of geography.

7-10 NAME THAT CONTINENT (K-3)

Objective: After completing this activity the student should be able to demonstrate a knowlege of land forms and geographic inquiry.

Materials Needed:

- world maps
- clue cards

Procedure:

1. Students should begin by dividing into teams. One member from each team negotiates a challenge by stating: "I can name that continent in _____ clues." No more than six clues may be bid. The other team member may choose to challenge by decreasing the amount of clues needed to identify the continent by stating, "I can name that continent in five clues." The first team may then opt to once again lower the amount of clues, or the challenge may be offered the opposing team to "name that continent."

2. The teacher then reads the clue cards which give a descriptor of the unnamed continent. If the challenged team identifies the continent correctly using the number of clues stated or less, they win a point. If, however, they fail to name the continent correctly, the opposing team then has the opportunity to answer. The challenging team may collectively have one minute to discuss the possibilities, then answer. If the response is correct, then they earn the point.

3. Suggestions: Students should make the clue cards by listing a minimum of eight descriptors about a continent beginning with general terms to the more concrete or obvious descriptors of a continent. This activity may be used with any study of maps or land forms.

7-11 GEOGRAPHICAL BINGO (4-6)

Objective: After completing this activity the student should be able to locate a land area using latitude and longitude.

Materials Needed:

- copies of "Geographical Bingo" maps
- markers
- teacher-made longitude/latitude cards

Procedure:

1. The teacher calls out the longitude and latitude. Students mark the location on their maps. The game proceeds until a student marks four consecutive boxes.
2. Once students have demonstrated mastery, they may use an atlas to write down the country or countries that were "marked" on their maps.

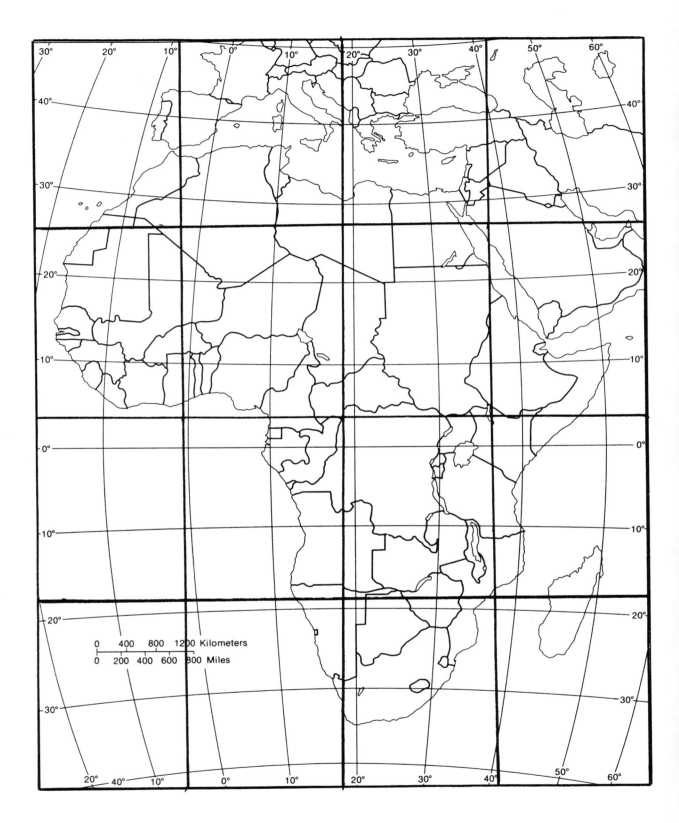

0 400 800 1200 Kilometers
0 200 400 600 800 Miles

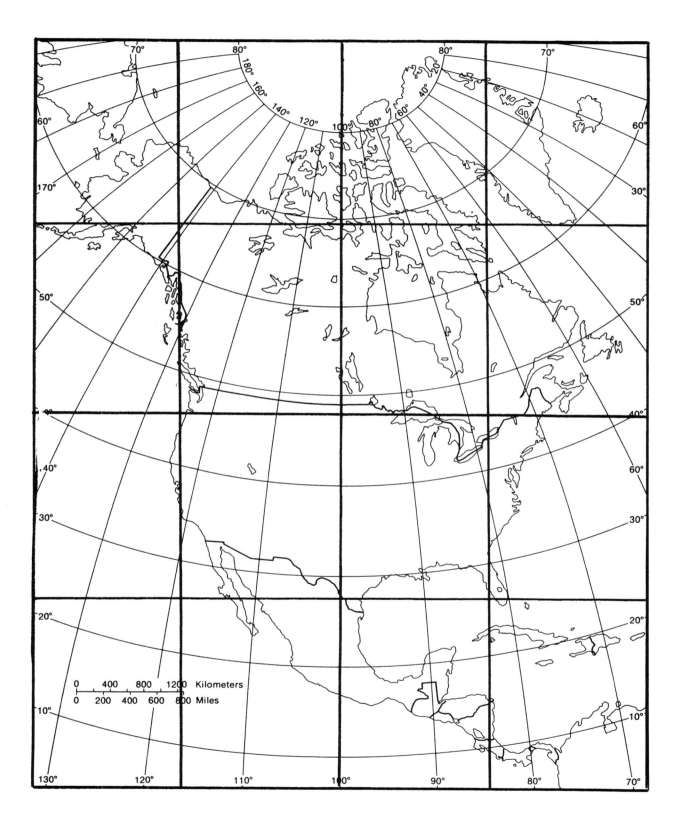

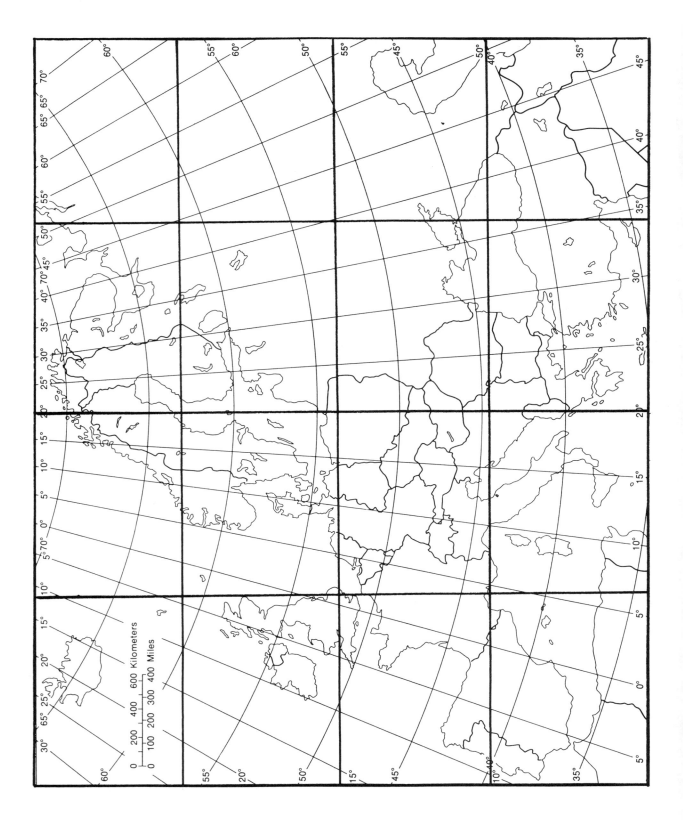

7-12 MAP FLUENCY (4-6)

Objective: After completing this activity the student should be able to use geographical vocabulary to describe an area of the earth.

Materials Needed:

- overhead projector
- transparencies of different maps
- copies of "Divisions of Geographical Sciences" sheet

Procedure:

1. Project the map transparency with a particular location highlighted. This may be an area previously studied, or if the students are not familiar with the highlighted area, an atlas book or encyclopedia may be used.
2. Students are then given three minutes to write descriptors of both physical geography and biogeography (see the geographical sciences sheet).
3. Students should list as many one- or two-word descriptors under each major section of physical geography and biogeography.
4. Dividing students into teams, let students have a two-minute time limit in which to name "round robin style" as many descriptors as possible. No team member may be skipped, so answers must be rapid and plentiful to accumulate points.

Name _____

DIVISIONS OF GEOGRAPHICAL SCIENCES

Physical Geography
(Land Forms)

_____

_____

_____

Mathematical Geography
(Meridians/Parallels)

_____

_____

_____

Meterology
(Weather/Temperature)

_____

_____

_____

Climatology
(Climate of the Area)

_____

_____

_____

_____

Plant Geography
(Plant Life)

_____

_____

_____

_____

Animal Geography
(Birds/Animals Native to the Area)

_____

_____

_____

Human Geography
(Demography, Economic Geography,
Political Geography, People,
Resources)

_____

_____

_____

7-13 THIS IS THE LAND THAT "JACK" BUILT (4-6)

Objective: After completing this activity the student should be able to correctly identify the relationships of factors relating to geography.

Materials Needed:

- large photographed pictures of major land features (examples: rivers, mountains, plains)

- pictures of people in various occupations; dwellings; animals; and vegetation

Procedure:

1. The pictures should be laid out on the floor. Students sit in a circle with one student beginning as "Jack." Jack chooses one large picture featuring a major earth feature and begins: "This is the (example: a picture of a river is chosen) river that runs through the land that Jack built." She/he then hands the picture to any student in the circle who would then choose a picture that would further "describe" Jack's land and state. "These are the people who live near the river that runs through the land that Jack built."

2. The procedure continues until all major components have been identified (e.g., land forms, major features, people, vegetation, climate, animals). Possible combinations are limited only by students' "justification" of choices.

Applied Geography

This exciting unit requires that students apply their knowledge of geography to unique problems.

7-14 PLANET X (4-6)

Objective: After completing this activity the student should be able to demonstrate an understanding of the various specialized fields of geography.

Materials Needed:

- large boxes
- clay
- glue
- yarn
- scissors

Procedure:

1. Introduce the activity by discussing how the students are to become specialists. Teams are to be formed with six members to a team. Each member becomes a specialized geographer and must design a portion of Planet X using data she/he has imaginatively collected from a geographer's viewpoint:

Demographer—prepares figures about populations (where people live, effects of births/deaths).

Climatologist—studies the effects of weather and its impact on the planet.

Oceanographer—explores a sea bottom to study plants and animals.

Animal Geographer—studies the types of animals and birds that inhabit an area.

Plant Geographer—studies the soil, weather, and other factors that affect plant life.

Physical Geographer—studies land forms such as mountains, plains, bodies of water.

2. The team will then construct a diorama using members' input to create a unique planet. (A diorama is a miniature scene that may be partially or wholly constructed in a three-dimensional manner to demonstrate a setting.) A written geographical account compiled by the members further enhances the display.

7-15 THE GREAT (FILL IN YOUR STATE'S NICKNAME) RACE (4-6)

Objective: After completing this activity the student should be able to read map scales/distance charts.

Materials Needed:

- state maps indicating cities and/ or roads
- acetate (type used for overhead projectors)

- water-soluble acetate marking pencils (three colors preferred)

Procedure:

1. Students may participate individually or in small groups. They must develop a travel plan across their state based on the following requirements:

—three types of transportation must be used (e.g., air, land and sea);

—the journey must include no more than 500 miles and not less than 300 miles, yet at least three major cities must be visited;

—the teacher adds the third requirement of a starting and finishing point.

2. Students indicate a code as to the type of transportation involved. The route is then plotted using the map scale of miles to calculate distances. (Plotting is drawn on acetate using water-soluble markers.)

3. The first student or team to correctly meet all requirements wins "The Great Race."

7-16 THE ABC's OF WORLD TRAVEL (4-6)

Objective: After completing this activity the student should be able to apply map reading and geographical inquiry skills to chart world travel.

Materials Needed:

- atlas
- balloons
- papier-mâché

- tempera paints
- world maps (polar projections work well for this activity)

Procedure:

1. Students will divide into small groups of six students. Each group will be assigned a letter, A, B, C, etc. The students are asked to plot a trip around the world using those countries or cities which begin with their assigned letter.

2. Each team member can be assigned to research one of the following:

   —type of land (topography) over which the team traveled

   —type of population patterns in the traveled lands

   —type of vegetation/animals found in the traveled lands

   —type of climate

   —type of products/resources found

   —type of transportation necessary to travel through each land

3. Reports of the travel adventure can be shared with the class. Globes may be constructed using balloons, papier-mâché, and tempera paints. The teams' world travel can then be plotted with string.

RESEARCH TOPICS FOR FURTHER STUDY OF "VIEWPOINTS"

Presented here are a collection of research topics for students seeking further challenges. The topics are designed to encourage higher-level thinking. *Beware:* young researchers may end up detouring into uncharted waters of knowldege and study. Nurture these departures.

1. Compare and contrast the life styles of early Indians with that of present Indians. Identify a minimum of three aspects of life that have not changed.

2. Investigate the life and times of a major river in your state. Attempt to include several historical accounts of life that were influenced by the river.

3. Select a famous mountain range of the world. Where is it in location to where you live? Imagine that you are planning to traverse the range. Explore what gear and travel arrangements you would need to be prepared. Call a travel agent to identify a possible itinerary.

4. Investigate an ideal vacation spot. Develop plans for traveling to this ideal vacation spot.

5. Explore the differences between two maps of the U.S. Identify how they are different. Share your results.

6. Develop a resource file of important people and famous quotations.

7. Identify ten famous women who achieved greatness. Investigate their backgrounds. What qualities did they share which propelled them into the arena of greatness?

BIBLIOGRAPHY FOR "VIEWPOINTS"

Creative Teaching of the Social Studies in the Elementary School by James A. Smith (Boston: Allyn and Bacon, 1967).

Illustrated Atlas of the Modern World (Danbury, CT: Warwick Press, 1981).

Lands and Peoples (New York: Grolier, Inc., 1983).

Maptime...U.S.A. by Jerry Aten (Carthage, IL: Good Apple, 1982).

Social Science Projects You Can Do by Thomas P. Weinland and Donald W. Protheroe (Englewood Cliffs, NJ: Prentice-Hall, 1973).

Windows to the World by Nancy Everix (Carthage, IL: Good Apple, 1982).